NEW DIRECTIONS
FOR EXPERIENTIAL
LEARNING

Number 11   •   1981

NEW DIRECTIONS FOR EXPERIENTIAL LEARNING

A Quarterly Sourcebook
Pamela J. Tate, Editor-in-Chief
Morris T. Keeton, Consulting Editor
Sponsored by the Council for the Advancement of
Experiential Learning (CAEL)

Number 11, 1981

Cross-Cultural Learning

Charles B. Neff
Guest Editor

Jossey-Bass Inc., Publishers
San Francisco • Washington • London

CROSS-CULTURAL LEARNING
New Directions for Experiential Learning
Number 11, 1981
   Charles B. Neff, Guest Editor

New Directions for Experiential Learning is published quarterly
by Jossey-Bass Inc., Publishers. Subscriptions are available
at the regular rate for institutions, libraries, and agencies
of $30 for one year. Individuals may subscribe at the special
professional rate of $18 for one year.

Correspondence:
Subscriptions, single-issue orders, change of address notices,
undelivered copies, and other correspondence should be sent to
New Directions Subscriptions, Jossey-Bass Inc., Publishers,
433 California Street, San Francisco, California 94104.

Editorial correspondence should be sent to the Editor-in-Chief,
Pamela J. Tate or the Consulting Editor, Morris T. Keeton
at the Council for the Advancement of Experiential Learning (CAEL),
Suite 300, Lakefront North, Columbia, Maryland 21044.

Library of Congress Catalogue Card Number LC 80-84274

International Standard Serial Number ISSN 0271-0595

International Standard Book Number ISBN 87589-826-2

Cover design by Willi Baum

Manufactured in the United States of America

Contents

v

Publications Available from CAEL:

Assessing Occupational Competences — A CAEL Handbook, Amiel Sharon
College-Sponsored Experiential Learning — A CAEL Handbook, John Duley and Sheila Gordon
College-Sponsored Experiential Learning — A CAEL Student Guide, Hadley and Nesbitt
"Developing and Expanding Cooperative Education," *New Directions for Experiential Learn-ing,* number 2, Pamela J. Tate and Morris T. Keeton, Editors
Efficient Evaluation of Individual Performance in Field Placement, Stephen L. Yelon and John S. Duley
Lifelong Learning: Purposes and Priorities, K. Patricia Cross

*Cross-cultural learning is not new, but questions about what it means
still need answers. Several questions are posed here which consider
what can be learned in cross-cultural situations, assessment
of the experience, and credit for the experience.*

Introduction:
Cross-Cultural Encounters

Charles B. Neff

The urge to encounter other cultures and to puzzle about their meaning is a
deep-rooted instinct in us all. In addition to pure wanderlust and perhaps the
even deeper desire to explore the limits of the unknown, there seem to be other
motives that explain the important place accorded to cross-cultural learning.
One is individual learning by oneself for oneself, by which one discovers how
"different" people behave differently and why they do so. The urge to expand
one's own world explains at least in part the old British presumption that education was not complete without the Continental Tour.

But the British did not send their educated elite abroad merely to make
them genteel persons. Like any other country, Britain had some national self-
interest at stake. In part, one needed to learn about other cultures because
one's neighbors could be enemies as well as friends. The better one understood
their habits and instincts, the better one was able to defend oneself against
them.

The West added another reason for placing a high value on encounters
with other cultures: One learns about differences in other people in order to
serve them better. Missionaries, who worked to convert and educate the
heathen, could perform their evangelical tasks only by learning more about
those whom they wished to enlighten. That instinct was quite different from
the one that had motivated those who carried out the Crusades, a movement
that had at its heart the desire to stamp out the infidel, not to understand him
or bring him to your side. Generations of missionaries to Africa and Asia
learned about foreign cultures before they went abroad. The Summer Insti-

tute of Linguistics pioneered research into exotic languages so that distant and obscure native groups would be able to comprehend the Bible.

Beginning in the early twentieth century, a different, more global motive led to a resurgence of interest in encounters with other cultures. If men and women could know each other on personal terms, it was argued, those personal links would begin to transcend and transform the squabbles between nations that can lead to war. International personal contacts were perceived as a way of achieving world peace. The Experiment in International Living (an organization in Brattleboro, Vermont), Youth for Understanding, and the American Field Service epitomize that ideal.

Whereas intercultural contacts have been thought of mainly in an international context, a new notion gained currency as the findings of social science came to be reflected in public policy. Why not attempt to deal with the differences in culture within your own national boundaries? Out of that realization came such programs as VISTA, the University Year for Action, the Cross-Cultural Field Study Program at Justin Morrill College of Michigan State University, and numerous others that attempted to interact with and learn from the subcultures that comprise the United States. Cross-cultural learning, which started "abroad," returned home to the barrio or to the block next door.

Cross-Cultural Learning: The Domain

In various ways, the chapters that follow explore the uniqueness of cross-cultural learning as one form of experiential learning. A culture consists of the interactions and communication patterns of people, the behavior which those people exhibit in that context, the artifacts that reflect their values, and the rewards and punishments that they receive for adherence to or deviation from the standard norms. Experiential learning has been given a succinct definition by Keeton and Tate (1978), as learning "in which the learner is directly in touch with the realities being studied." They contrasted it with "learning in which the learner only reads about, hears about, talks about, or writes about realities but never comes in contact with them as part of the learning process." Cross-cultural experiential learning, then, is learning that occurs as a result of being in direct contact with a culture other than one's own.

A great deal has been written, particularly in recent years, about the need properly to acknowledge and assess learning that derives from experience and to accord to it the same regard and rewards we give to traditional classroom education (Keeton and Associates, 1976; Duley, 1974). The experiential education movement has forced us all to take a fresh look at some of our assumptions. It has, for instance, caused us to look more closely at the time factor. Can we give credits only to education that occurs in the present or that will be obtained in a traditional standardized way in the future? Is it not fair to look at past experience and to assess the learning that has occurred, independently of its connection with formal education? Similarly, most of what we call education occurs in formal settings, organized by colleges, universities, industry, government, and the armed services. Is that the only way we learn? Is there not also a form of entirely personalized learning that occurs independently of the classroom setting and also deserves some recognition? Are poems written by a person who has found a published outlet for them less worthy of college credit than poems that are written in a creative writing class?

Some experiences are work related, while others are not. Does the fact that work is associated with a learning experience rule out academic credit for that experience?

But there is yet another type of question that will be addressed in the following chapters. Is the experience with another culture qualitatively different from other types of experiential learning? If so, in what way is it different? Can we assume that acquaintance with another culture is a learning experience of sufficient import to merit educational credit, even if that acquaintance is as fleeting and superficial as a tourist junket? If tourism seems inadequate to provide a college-level experience, what do we mean by an adequate acquaintance with another culture? Is it the length of the encounter? Is it a skill, like language or ability to deal with strange situations? Is it a process of personal change, of increased idealism? If we can define the adequacy of acquaintance, how do we measure that adequacy and how do we balance it with traditional college credit norms?

Designing the Experience: What Should Be Learned?

Recently, a group jointly sponsored by the Council on International Educational Exchange (CIEE) and Michigan State University (MSU) assembled for the purpose of assessing current practices in experiential learning and cross-cultural programs. The general statement developed by this group read in part as follows: "Cross-cultural experiential learning can be defined as the acquisition of skills, knowledge, and competencies through a learner's contact with and reflection upon the direct realities of a host society. . . . Cross-cultural experiential education is preeminently integrative in nature. The student connects with the host culture at all levels of his being. Such programs offer opportunities for the acquisition of factual knowledge, for synthesizing data, determining patterns of meaning, developing powers of independent observation, and for the application of knowledge and understanding to the immediate situations at hand. At the same time, the student is provided opportunities for greater self-confidence, awareness, and understanding of his or her own culture and values; for the testing of effective patterns in interacting with people and situations; and a corresponding potential for the development of personal maturity and capacities in the learning process itself" ["Statement of the Task Group . . . ," 1979].

This statement is helpful in describing the general domain of experiential learning in a cross-cultural setting, and it is a useful first step in helping us to define the type of learning that should be properly supported and rewarded in the educational process. The next step is to be precise about what is desirable in cross-cultural experiential education.

The CIEE/MSU group also suggests that, ideally, experiential cross-cultural learning programs will be based on certain program components, including "maximum contact with the new social environment, clear learning objectives, opportunities for the discovery of the culture by the students, [and] subjecting the experience to intellectual examination and reflection" ("Statement of the Task Group . . . ," 1979).

In an earlier volume in this series of sourcebooks that dealt with the measurement of competence in experiential learning (Klemp, 1979), George Klemp provided a definition of competence and further divided the components of competence into the following: knowledge, skill, trait, self-schema, and motive.

Drawing on Klemp's definition, the CIEE/MSU list could be redefined in the cross-cultural context to specify our expectations of students prior to engaging in the learning process and the desirable outcomes of that process (see Table 1).

This may not be the best way of depicting the desired outcomes of experientially based cross-cultural learning, but some definition of desirable competency is called for initially.

Table 1.

	Preexperience	*Postexperience*
Knowledge	Adequate knowledge of the other culture in general terms and specific knowledge of any of its parts (for example, local government, art museums) with which the student will have contact.	Measurable increase in knowledge of the same aspects of the other culture; addition of knowledge about other aspects.
Skill	Minimal fluency in a language of the other culture. Demonstrated sensitivity to changes in behavior required by the host culture. Ability to articulate motive(s) for the cross-cultural experience.	Measurable increase in fluency. Increased sensitivity and ability to analyze the changes that actually occurred. Ability to analyze the effect of motive on the experience and to describe any resulting changes.
Trait	Willingness to tolerate cultural differences. Willingness to seek an integrated understanding of another culture through direct experience of it.	Willingness to reflect upon and integrate the experience in personal and intellectual terms.
Self-schema	Perception of oneself as open and able to learn from a cross-cultural experience.	Perception of oneself as having learned from the cross-cultural experience and as capable of learning from other such experiences.
Motive	Any one or more of several, including to learn, to acquire language skills, to increase international understanding.	Desire to maintain sustained contact with the same culture or with a different culture.

Assessing the Experience: What Is Learned?

When we have decided what is desirable, the next step is to develop the assessment techniques that can tell us what kind of learning has occurred. In other words, what do we know or not know about the learning which has occurred in the area or areas that we have designated as important?

Assessment techniques vary in their degree of development and acceptance by the general academic community. Almost any kind of factual knowledge can be assessed by some kind of examination. Although there is still considerable debate about what constitutes a proper examination and whether examinations properly assess the learning they purport to measure, by and large, there will be less debate in this area than in any other, and there are many standard instruments that can be used. If a student is asked to analyze the power structure of a community or the economic import of a particular region for a foreign country, we could with relative confidence design an instrument to measure the factual knowledge that he or she has acquired in evaluating the entities or processes that he or she has examined.

Skills are slightly more difficult, although not impossible, to assess. Language usage in a foreign culture is the principal necessary skill, and in assessing it we find ourselves on firm ground. There are numerous ways, many of them standardized, such as the Foreign Service Institute Examination, for determining the progress that a student has made in language acquisition. Language acquisition, however, may be only a part of the learning that we are trying to encourage. How is the language used? Is it used effectively in all kinds of situations? Is it used only for basic communications? Does it become a coping skill that allows the student to solve an evolving series of problems, beginning at a simple level (seeking directions) and ending at a much more complex level (explaining differences between cultures to a person from the other culture)? Do we expect the outcome of language acquisition to be a fairly mechanical one; that is, can the student control a symbol system or dialect that is foreign? Or are we more concerned with the student's ability to use that language for particular purposes; that is, to get around more easily in a foreign setting or to be able to communicate complex ideas more effectively in a foreign culture? Assessment of the language skill might merely measure what the student could do (if placed in position X with desired purpose Y, the student could produce desired outcome Z) when what we perhaps wish to measure is that he or she in fact does produce that outcome in any given situation (for instance, placed in a situation where there is misunderstanding, he or she can use language to produce greater understanding).

Thus, if the acquisition of coping skills is a desirable outcome, the assessment of those skills moves us gradually away from the skills themselves and into other areas that are far more difficult to measure. Yet these very areas often serve as the justification for programs involving study in other cultures.

Integration of the experience with knowledge acquired earlier or modification of previous values by the experience is often cited as a desirable outcome. But what kind of integration do we wish to promote? The same kind in every student asking that equal weight be given to increased knowledge or enhanced coping skills by each individual? If that seems undesirable, what kind of individualized recognition can be accorded the integration of the experience before, during, and after a cross-cultural encounter?

Empathy presents another kind of assessment problem. Its measurement is not impossible but is a more difficult task than measurement of the skills themselves, of factual knowledge, or even of integration. Some research has been done on measuring competencies in empathy (for instance, the work of McBer Associates in Cambridge, Massachusetts), although little, if anything, has been done to isolate assessment of those particular traits in a cross-cultural setting. Can we assume that a person who is empathic within his own culture will, given the proper skills, also be empathic in a cross-cultural setting? If we make empathy one goal of a program, what are we doing to increase empathy, beyond placing students in situations where they must demonstrate that quality in order to get along?

If language and empathy are difficult although not impossible to measure, both as coping skills and as more broadly defined communication skills, we enter an even more difficult area when we talk about *personal development,* another frequently mentioned justification for cross-cultural learning. Evidently, most people who engage in cross-cultural learning say that the experience is a "good one" and that it has "changed" them as people, while many say also that they have developed a lasting commitment to cross-cultural understanding on one form or another. Outside observers will say that someone has returned as a "different person." But how do we assess these changes and what kind of value do we place upon them? Is personal development in a cross-cultural setting different from personal development in general? Do we need to assess it at all?

Crediting the Experience: How Much Is the Learning Worth?

These points have led us to the third area of major concern. If we know what outcomes are desirable and how to assess them, which of those outcomes should be rewarded and in what way? In academic terms, that means the kind of credit that we give. In some areas, we find ourselves on very firm ground. Factual knowledge can be equated with courses. We can find some tool in our interdisciplinary bag of tricks to measure certain types of integration, particularly at the intellectual level. But what about the other areas — the broader communication skills of language and empathy, personal development and commitment? Should they be given academic credit? If the experience itself is not what we are rewarding, what forms of learning among all those that occur should be given some formal educational recognition? If personal development is not given academic credit in traditional settings, should it be given credit in cross-cultural settings? Would we expect to give some kind of pretest on intellectual, emotional, and ethical development before immersion in another culture, to be followed by a posttest at the conclusion of the experience? This is clearly impractical, and it would probably not be of much value, since development occurs over long periods of time, and the effects of an experience may manifest themselves quite late in a person's development.

Fortunately, there are some preliminary answers to these questions. Leaving aside the acquisition of knowledge or of specific skills such as language, which are both relatively easy to measure and considered legitimately rewardable in conventional academic terms, some precedents exist for rewarding the other, less easily measurable parts of a cross-cultural experience.

In general, these precedents point to mixed assessment, evaluating knowledge and skills as we usually do, but subjecting the rest of the experience to a holistic overview. John Duley, for instance, has described in detail how one program assesses a cross-cultural experience in terms of seven specific characteristics using a "critical incident" methodology (Duley, 1974). Similarly, Joan Knapp and Amiel Sharon give an example of "product assessment," showing how the experience of a student individually studying "the history, art, and culture of the host country by visiting museums, art galleries, and architectural landmarks" can be evaluated for academic credit (Knapp and Sharon, 1975). Stephen Yelon and John Duley have listed techniques that can be employed in holistic evaluation, giving examples and discussing the advantages and problems (Yelon and Duley, 1978).

Contributions to This Volume

The contributors to this volume do not answer all the questions asked here, but they do extend our understanding of cross-cultural experiential education in some important ways.

Michael J. Flack points out that the term *experience* has at least three separate meanings — practical wisdom, history, and direct observation of or participation in events. He relates these three different meanings to the concept of learning and to attempts in the last few decades to integrate experience in one of its several forms with the learning process. He uses illustrations to remind us that the effects of experiential learning upon a single individual as a "cultural isolate" are quite different from the effect of experience upon groups. This is especially true when the group learns to reinforce itself or to interact in ways that extend its experience to other groups, which, instead of remaining isolated from and disinterested in the reported experience, can partake of it in a secondary fashion. Finally, he discusses the fact that cross-cultural experiential learning need not be limited to experiences abroad but can also take place among the subcultures of our own society. By addressing the theory of cross-cultural experiential learning in a theoretical and historical way, he expands for us the educational context within which we should consider its consequences.

Robert Pearson surveys the research that has been done on the effects of experiential learning in cross-cultural settings. He warns us that all contacts do not necessarily produce what we would call favorable results. He also reminds us that, although we generally attempt to produce favorable results by manipulating the environment within which the individual has his or her experience, it is often the variables which define the individual prior to the experience that have at least as great an effect on the outcomes as the environment itself. He surveys specific experiments and assessment studies, which he relates to some general conclusions about the role of assessment in experiential learning.

Joseph Axelrod discusses one specialized aspect of cross-cultural experiential learning, the role of language. He generalizes from the actual experience of a single individual to arrive at conclusions about three important contributions of language to the learning process: language as the medium of basic communication, language as a way of seeing a culture from within, and language as an important influence on affective changes. These conclusions lead to further discussion of the "curious relationship" between knowledge of language and knowledge of culture. He concludes with an analysis of the amount of language that is needed to enhance experiential learning.

Martin Tillman deals with the practical experience of the Lisle Fellowship, a small but significant group, which has a long and continuous experience with cross-cultural experiential learning and with a unique means of organizing its groups. Tillman also reflects on the experience, and in many cases the difficulties, that he has had in translating a nontraditional way of learning into the traditional currency of academic credit. Discussion of the means for enhancing the experience of groups (a practical explication of some of the theoretical points made earlier by Michael Flack) leads Tillman to some observations on assessment and rewards.

Finally, Irwin Abrams, an experienced practitioner in the area of cross-cultural experiential learning, addresses issues not only of design (the degree to which cross-cultural experiential learning should resemble traditional programs; how much supervision is needed in the field) and program operation (preexperience activities, organization of the program in the field, group and individual relations with the host culture) but also the means by which the experience can be maximized after reentry into the home culture. In the process, he offers some very practical advice about the homestay, work experience, and independent study. His checklist of twelve points could be used by any program planner to ensure that important points for planning and implementation have not been overlooked.

To conclude the volume, a brief statement by the editor considers some of the issues that have yet to be addressed thoroughly or resolved and that form an agenda for the future in promoting the cause of cross-cultural experiential learning.

References

Duley, J. "Cross-Cultural Field Study." In J. Duley (Ed.), *New Directions for Higher Education: Implementing Field Experience Education*, no. 6. San Francisco: Jossey-Bass, 1974.

Keeton, M. T., and Tate, P. J. (Eds.). *New Directions for Experiential Learning: Learning by Experience: What, Why, How*, no. 1. San Francisco: Jossey-Bass, 1978.

Keeton, M. T., and Associates. *Experiential Learning: Rationale, Characteristics, and Assessment*. San Francisco: Jossey-Bass, 1976.

Klemp, G. O., Jr. "Identifying, Measuring, and Integrating Competence." In P. S. Pottinger and J. Goldsmith (Eds.), *New Directions for Experiential Learning: Defining and Measuring Competence*, no. 3. San Francisco: Jossey-Bass, 1979.

Knapp, J., and Sharon, A. *A Compendium of Assessment Techniques*. Cooperative Assessment of Experiential Learning and Educational Testing Service, 1975.

"Statement of the Task Group on the Role of Experiential Learning in Cross-Cultural Programs." Michigan State University, mimeograph, March 1979. (Available from John Duley, Learning and Evaluation Service, 17 Morrill Hall, Michigan State University, East Lansing, Michigan 48824.)

Yelon, S. L., and Duley, J. S. *Efficient Evaluation of Individual Performance in Field Placement.* Guides for the Improvement of Instruction in Higher Education, no. 14. East Lansing: Michigan State University, 1978.

Charles B. Neff was formerly associate vice-chancellor for international programs of the State University of New York, where this sourcebook was edited. He also served as director of educational programs for the Peace Corps in Colombia and for thirteen years was at the University of Hawaii. He is currently president of the Associated Colleges of the Midwest (A.C.M.), in Chicago. A.C.M. is a consortium of thirteen liberal arts colleges (Beloit, Carleton, Coe, Colorado, Cornell, Grinnell, Knox, Lake Forest, Lawrence, Macalester, Monmouth, Ripon, and St. Olaf) with strong international programs administered by the separate colleges and the consortium as a whole.

*"Experience" is given different meanings. How we define it and
how it has been interpreted in the past shape our world view
and the learning we derive from cross-cultural encounters.
Experience also differs to the extent that it emphasizes
the individual or the group.*

Experiential Learning in Transnational Contexts

Michael J. Flack

Experience—the core concept in *experiential*—carries three separate meanings,
according to Webster's dictionary.

First, it refers to an accumulated practical wisdom, skill, or competence deriving from extended participation in a particular activity or profession. For example, we speak of the *experienced* diplomat, teacher, commander,
planner, surgeon.

Second, it point to the sum total of events that make up the past of a
community or a nation or that have occurred within the knowledge of mankind generally and to the meaning and lessons attributed to that past or knowledge. For example, *Experience counsels that if one wants peace, one should prepare for
war.*

Third, it refers to direct observation or participation in events, an
encountering, undergoing, or living through things in general as they take
place in the course of time. Here, *experiencing* is a process or method involving
a more or less conscious activation of awareness.

The separateness of these three meanings is heuristically questionable,
for in each case the concept involves the results, lessons, or process of exposure
to realizations or perceptions about what is, has been, or should be, with applications relating to the quality of practice, the content and implications of the
record, or the process by which abstract notions are tested and revised. In all
three cases, that is, the underlying notion is that of learning—through practice, the presentation of history, and direct personal involvement.

Some thirty-five years ago, John Dewey (1937) formulated an incisive rationale for the experiential component in education when he characterized experience as including of necessity "an active and a passive element peculiarly combined." The active element involved "trying," the passive, "undergoing." And, he continued, "We do something to the thing and then it does something to us in return. Such is the peculiar combination. The connection of these two phases of experience measures the fruitfulness or value of the experience. Mere activity does not constitute experience. It is dispersive, centrifugal, dissipating. Experience as trying involves change, but change is meaningless transition unless it is consciously connected with the return wave of consequences which flow from it. When an activity is continued *into* the undergoing of consequences, when the change made by action is reflected back into change made in us, the mere flux is loaded with significance. We learn something" (Dewey, 1937, p. 163).

As is often the case with concepts and innovations, Dewey was arguing against a practice deemed unsatisfactory. The target was an objectified, bookish, memory-focused, mechanistic, and grade-oriented pedagogy that all too often, as one wit put it, involved "the transfer of notes from those of the professor to those of the student without going through the mind of either." Exaggerated as this characterization may be, traditional pedagogy tended to focus on a predefined subject matter, on the class, on the often didactic presentation of ready-made knowledge, or on rationalization rather than on the individual student, the student's motivation, the discovery and construction of pertinence, and learning as the incorporation and transformation of the biographical into the general and vice versa.

The immediate thrust of the experiential proposition was the available social environment: the conception of the city as a multifaceted, readily available resource; of field experience as confrontation with live actors and organizations; of concrete or participant observation as the comprehension of operating models in situations, organizations, and action. All this was both feasible and reachable. If permitted or approved, it could be done. Nor was it meant completely to replace the traditional approaches. The book, the exercise, the lecture, and the grading continued — with occasional ventures into experience or invitations to report on or engage in self-confrontation or self-learning that represented a diversification and enrichment of the curricular norm.

There was more recourse to self-learning in some fields than in others: Physics and chemistry regularly involved laboratory experiments; zoology, the dissection of frogs and snakes; and social work and medicine, involvement in activities appropriate to junior understudies in practicum or internship roles. Others could test their creativity in poetry workshops and dramatic productions, and still others in the increasing opportunities for summer internships or employment or as graduate, research, or teaching assistants in educational institutions. The environment to be invaded was less formal and standardized than the classroom, but even so it was restricted by the location of the institution, by use of the national language, and by the availability of funds. Thus, the focus was socially local and sociologically domestic.

Of course, there were opportunities for foreign sojourns and study or for the presence of students or teachers from abroad. In broad perspective, however, these were neither very regular nor plannable, they did not involve large numbers of participants, and, beyond the generalized rhetoric about international understanding, they were only rarely thought of as involving experiential education. Then as now, the rub of cultures and nationalities, even in the most intimate of class environments, tended to remain ad hoc and superficial, defining differences as quaint rather than as generic and absorbing them within the expectation, often internalized by the visitor, that he or she should adjust to the host country's folkways; that is, that he or she should become a temporary *us* rather than function as an exponent of a different culture and of different values and virtues.

World War II, which was much more global than its predecessor; the return of millions of G.I.'s who had served and won abroad; the infusion into American life and especially into education of a considerable number of outstanding foreign scholars and researchers; and the comprehensive embrace by government, academia, and the public of the need for a new type of world, a functioning United Nations, and democracy within and among peoples all produced a change. The number of foreign students who came to study in the U.S. increased from 26,759 in 1948-49 to 263,938 in 1978-79, and the number of American students studying abroad, while it lags far behind, increased from 9,457 in 1954-55 to 34,218 in 1971-72 and it is now estimated by the Statistical Research Division of the Institute of International Education in New York to number 50,000 or more persons.

New ventures like the Fulbright (later the Fulbright-Hays) Program, the State Department's Leader and Specialist Program, a variety of international organization fellowships including U.N.E.S.C.O., considerable growth in foundation, church-related, unilateral and bilateral university programs, and the like expanded the number, structure, and type of exchanges of persons and the types of experience that they had.

Two other factors had major impact: first, the growing preoccupation with development reflected in the considerable number of bureaucrats, experts, university personnel, and Peace Corps personnel stationed abroad for long terms, and, of course, AID and counterpart government-sponsored training and education programs; and second, the disintegration after 1957 of the imperial world and its rapid replacement by the present system of some 160 independent nations, almost 100 of them new to sovereign statehood. Both factors resulted in a growing awareness in the public consciousness of the facts of multiculturality; of the existence, normality, and legitimacy of diversity; of the need to cooperate as partners with peoples formerly known largely from postage stamps or Tarzan movies; and ultimately of the constraining imperative of interdependence. All these, in diffuse ways, demanded a review of America's self-concept and of its place in the world: From the periphery of a variously unenlightened and strife-torn world, the United States became one of the major members and animators of that world, which demanded to be taken seriously, more fully heeded, and more systematically known, studied, and appreciated. This difficult reorientation and redefinition continues into our own day.

Experience of the international realm can encompass the world as a whole with knowledge, attitudes, and orientations to it; other countries and societies; and the bases and values on which the mutual interrelationships among them are or should be posited.

In the concrete and empirical sense of the word, it is obvious that no one can experience "the world." It is too large and too diversified to become accessible to the biological and psychological limitations of adult life. In a more restricted sense, however, there are persons who, professionally or by decision, have managed to build into their lives enough exposure to other societies that they may in a general sense be said to have acquired world experience. Career diplomats, personnel of international organizations, missionaries, and members of other international auxiliary services fit the professional category. Those who have acquired such experience by decision are philosophers of highly evolved empathy and vision who have set out to absorb the globe's variety into their consciousness. Count Hermann Keyserling's two-volume *Diary of a Traveling Philosopher* is the record of such an enterprise. Most people, however, manage exposure to one or very few other societies, but even this can have a profound effect on world view. Edmond Taylor's *Richer by Asia* is a sterling report on such experience.

This sourcebook focuses on the student years and on the experiential learning that can be associated with the years of advanced education and training. Thus, the restricted sense in which both professionals and philosophers can be said to have world experience can be excluded. Instead, attention will be directed to the period of learning in which formal institutional curricula and core requirements permit varying degrees of diversification both in subject matter and in technique. The experiential learning approach is one avenue for such diversification.

Years ago, Dorwin Cartwright (1951) drew attention to the cultural bias that animated much American educational thought about the ways in which people change their behavior or resist efforts by others to have them do so: "I have become convinced that no small part of the trouble has resulted from an irresistible tendency to conceive of our problems in terms of the individual. We live in an individualistic culture. We value the individual highly, and rightly so. But I am inclined to believe that our political and social concern for the individual has narrowed our thinking as social scientists so much that we have not been able to state our research problem properly. Perhaps we have taken the individual as the unit of observation and study when some larger unit would have been more appropriate" (Cartwright, 1951, p. 383).

Citing empirical research, by now much multiplied, Cartwright points to the group as a potent source of influence on attitudinal or operational change in its members and on the prospect that such change may continue and become effective in social application. "The approach to training which conceives of its task as being merely that of changing the individual probably produces frustration, demoralization, and disillusionment in as large a measure as it accomplishes more positive results" (Cartwright, 1951, p. 386).

This is relevant to experiential learning in the international and intercultural context in three ways.

First, the major part of experiential learning is generally thought of as the result of an individual sojourning student's subjective and objective exposure to behaviors in the society in which he or she is the temporary resident and participant. As R. D. Laing defines it (1967, p. 17), "The task of social phenomenology is to relate my experience of the other's behavior. Its study is the relation between experience and experience: its true field is *interexperience.*" In this sense, exposure involving social phenomenological exchanges can enhance empathy, understanding of the logic behind the cultural pattern, and ability to function within it.

The question is whether this personal exposure to a different cultural context promotes learning of a second culture, with its postulates and requirements, without necessarily affecting the core structure of the visitor's native culture. The assumption that sojourners abroad learn new behavioral patterns and values that affect or replace old ones—as if the human mind were a single place where only a single cultural pattern can reside at one time—is dubious indeed. Rather, what often evolves is a kind of parallel existence of two operational cultures—one original, affective, and comforting in such basic realms as religion, food, personal ethics, music, friendship, and style of expression; the other secondary, learned by coping with the host environment, functional but partial and role- and problem-related, and animated by the need to be adequate and effective in the new context. Whether this amounts to a type of situational cultural schizophrenia or to a double larder of social and cultural resources and valuations is not an issue for argument, for it varies with the person, the "distance" between the two cultures, and the status sought or defended. Above all, it varies with the visitor's degree of continued commitment to his or her own society, the determination to return, and the maintenance of intensive communicational and professional links with home.

The pertinent point is this: The experiential learning by the foreign individual as an individual, or, as Cartwright puts it, as a "cultural isolate," may be only partially applicable to the role that he or she is to play upon return home. Unless there is support by a critical mass of colleagues with similar experiences and broadened cultural registers, the individual may soon relegate a good portion of the new experience to latent or dormant status. We have all experienced the awkwardness that enthusiastic travelers feel when the slides that they present to their friends on return—so meaningful to them as recollections of what they had seen and experienced—evoke only polite boredom.

For experiential learning to carry over into the postreturn situation, for it to serve as a constantly active, rewarded competence or skill, there is need of receptivity to new ideas and overt appreciation of the experience abroad at home, in the university, or in the organization to which the individual returns. Such factors affect whether the experience becomes a residue of skills and understandings or continues to be employed as an alternative cultural register in an enlarged vision of task meeting and life itself.

Such reinforcement can come only from groups that are not generally present or that are reluctant to include the returnee in their ranks. In a study of the extensive research literature on foreign students (Spaulding and Flack, 1976, p. 289), we pointed to the great importance and influence exercised in this respect by conational foreign student groups on campuses of American universities and by alumni groups.

Second, experiential learning is often programmed and discussed as involving groups of students, sometimes recruited from a single institution, sometimes recruited nationwide. Two chapters in this sourcebook describe such approaches. Once recruited, the group usually undergoes preparatory orientation, which may be cognitive, behavioral, or both. Next, the group becomes aware of and comes to share the overall objective of the project; engages in a parallel program of formal and informal study; acquires information; partakes — as a group or as subgroups — of experiential forays, contacts, and exposures within the host culture; affords opportunities for idiosyncratic experiences by individual members; develops personal and collective friendships; and learns, at random and by plan, about the host society and nation and, to varying degrees, about the processes and implications of the host culture.

A considerable number of evaluative studies report that such experience was valuable and appreciated and that new knowledge and learning as well as new interests, realizations, likes, and dislikes resulted from it. Almost always, the experience abroad results in a more differentiated and sophisticated perspective, not only on the host society but also, and importantly so, on one's own society. The first look at strangers often becomes a first look at ourselves, with the resultant assessments ranging from heightened cultural nationalism and and appreciation for the home culture to a more critical view of its behaviors and values. Most returnees to the United States and the other industrially developed countries tend in this respect to locate and then move along the in-between area on a continuum running from total approval to disapproval of the home culture.

Third, however competently it has been planned and consummated and however much it includes elements of both cognitive and affective learning, experiential learning represents only an intermediate approach as regards the goal of immersion. This is particularly true if the group continues to use its national language while abroad in instruction, in contacts, and in the group's interchanges and assessment of its members' collective and individual experiences. While this author is not seeking to downgrade such ventures, it is true that they sometimes assume the character of educational excursions, a literal semester or year abroad, where only some visiting foreign teachers, the ambiance of the foreign town and travel, the temporary focus on learning about some aspects of the host culture, and the pleasure of foreign food, new friends, and frequent travel make the difference between what occurs and what would have occurred on the home campus. Figure 1 describes the well-integrated four-year program of Callison College at the University of the Pacific.

Not everyone can be exposed to experiential learning abroad. The locale of the individual's college studies may in some cases offer a valuable alternative. Let it be noted that international learning, as it is usually conceived, involves two dimensions: acquisition of cross-, inter-, and multicultural orientations and skills and acquisition of the facts and opportunities of the international world, together with their political, economic, social, and ideological implications. Both dimensions can be strongly supported by direct

Figure 1. Overseas Study

Typical Four-Year Sequence at Raymond-Callison College

University of the Pacific
(Related to Callison Year-in-Japan Program)

Freshman—Cultural Anthropology (4 units, required).
  Orientation to Cross-Cultural Learning (2 units, required).
  Japanese Language (4 units or one semester, required; two semesters strongly
    recommended. Intensive off-campus summer language program accepted).
  Area Course (4 units, one course required. Must be related to area of overseas
    study. Chosen from history, art, religion, anthropology, or political science.)

Sophomore—*Year Abroad* (Japan, Taiwan, India, Nepal possible).
  Divided into:
  Entry—A one-week general orientation in Kyoto, Japan.
  Phase I—Intensive Japanese Language. Student living with a Japanese family.
    Three months.
  Phase II—Internship or Cultural Track Tutorial. Continuation of home-stay
    family from Phase I.
  Interim—Week to ten-day travel break. Student must make arrangements, figure
    budget, travel, and report its outcome.
  Phase III—Academic instruction in Japanese university. Dormitory housing.
    Three months.

Junior—Reentry Seminar (2 units, required) in fall semester.
  Major retrospective paper assigned and various questionnaires administered.

Senior—International Studies seminar (4 units, required) in spring semester.
  Utilized as "capstone" course to four-year sequence.

Academic degrees granted under this program:
  1. B.A. in International Studies—*concentrations* in East Asia, Japan, or China
     (124 units)
  2. B.A. in International Studies—*majors* in East Asia or Comparative Cultures
     (132 units)

Dr. Bruce LaBrack
Raymond-Callison College
University of the Pacific

---

experience abroad. If direct experience abroad is not possible, however, at least some part of the first dimension can be developed in the home country. As Katherine Kendall has noted, "One does not need to cross an ocean or a national border to find people whose ideas, values, attitudes, and behavior seem different and alien. The many cultures and subcultures within a community, city, or country offer a number of possibilities for experiential cultural learning. . ." (Sikkema and Niyekawa-Howard, 1977, pp. iv–v).

To illustrate, this author can report that, for the past twenty years, he has had students in his course on intercultural analysis and operations visit a "strange" church in the city on the first week's Sunday (or Friday or Saturday, as the case may be) — not for religious reasons but for culture learning reasons. Students are urged to select a denomination that differs substantially in type and practice from their own. That is, students from religions with formal proceedings and rituals are encouraged to visit more spontaneous or revivalist services, while students from predominantly white, middle-class constituencies are urged to attend churches where the preacher and congregation are Blacks, Moslems, Hindus, Jews, spiritualists, or devotees of Krishna. Each student requests advance permission to attend — and then writes a three- to five-page report for the class on what happened and how it felt. The reports are revealing. Many students take their spouses or friends with them. They seem to face a moral problem from the feeling that they are participating as outsiders in what is a service for insiders. They react to specific religious or commercial elements in the proceedings and comment on the surroundings, sermon, money collection, types of persons attending, and behavior or "misbehavior" during the service. Most students indicate that they plan to visit other churches and denominations in following weeks. Except where deeply doctrine-oriented persons are involved, the reports and subsequent class discussion indicate a surprised, enhanced, and animated discovery of acceptance or respect for the other mode and a sense of the common factors underlying the external differences of form, garment, scent, language, and music.

This concrete motivating experience serves as a basis not only for extended class debate but also for a subsequent theory-developing "ordering" introduction by the instructor, which is welcomed by the students because it is felt to assist in the desired comprehension.

The whole course proceeds in this manner: Experience comes first, followed and assisted by explanatory conceptualization. As the course advances, the conceptual and theoretical components weave into a framework that carries increasingly into the anticipation, experience, and interpretation of the situations that are to be experienced.

The "strange" church tactic is one instance of this approach. Every instructor can survey the resources available in the community and the techniques by which these resources may be transformed into learning. Let it be mentioned that ethnic neighborhood centers, Black theaters, Salvation Army hostels, refugee camps, and the like as sites either for ad hoc field visits or for protracted, internship-like immersion in their living logic and process can provide students with experiential learning that is generically equivalent to what can be experienced from cultural exposure abroad. What we are referring to is the experience and resultant growth that comes from comprehending that the culture patterns of other groups, even within one's own society, seem functional, normal, natural, and cherished by their members. This, of course, is the essence of the intercultural proposition: that distinct human groups — whether they be nations, subgroups, or other in-groups in protracted intensive mutual interaction and communication — develop, learn, and transmit ways of life that serve the group as approaches and values in defining and coping with the objectives and challenges of social life. If one thinks of international relations as encompassing more than transactions of the governmental bureaucracies that advance and defend corporate national interests, then the intercultural proposition is the operationally essential base for the nonethnocentric, nonsuperior, and reciprocally cooperative attitude that is presupposed in the type of egalitarian relations which the United Nations charter identifies as "equal sovereignty" and which the postimperial ideology of the age subsumes as demands for equal dignity, rights, and representation.

To conclude: In the preceding pages, which have focused on the international dimensions and utility of experiential learning, the author defined experiential learning and sought to apply it in a number of forms and instances. He drew attention to the individual-group experience issue, particularly as it relates to reinforcement and duration of the change produced. The focus was restricted to the American university and its students — on campus, in the field, and abroad. Cross-cultural and internationalizing growth were the stated twin objectives.

The world is larger than this small component of mankind. The 1980 World Bank Report states that 850 million persons in developing countries lack basic education. Nevertheless, *experiential education,* a term often used interchangeably in the developing world with *experience-based education* or *training,* seems to be the call of the hour. The development of well-prepared managers, administrators, teachers, and social animators places increasing demands on universities and other institutions in such nations to evolve in-service training programs for government and the private realm, to minimize lectures, and to develop experience-based activities that could be utilized in classroom settings. This, of course, represents a public and social imperative, which seeks to produce not just properly schooled individuals but qualified, "whole" Nigerians, Senegalese, or Indonesians. The primary urgency is to produce competence for and on the broad, often multiethnic national level. This author hopes that it will not be long before the imperative for intercultural and international experience can also become the educational agenda for the rest of mankind.

References

Cartwright, D. "Achieving Change in People: Some Applications of Group Dynamics Theory." *Human Relations,* 1951, *4,* 381–392.

Dewey, J. *Democracy and Education.* New York: Macmillan, 1937.

Keyserling, H. *Travel Diary of a Philosopher.* Vols. 1 and 2. New York: Harcourt Brace, 1925.

Laing, R. D. *The Politics of Experience.* New York: Ballantine Books, 1967.

Sikkema, M., and Niyekawa-Howard, A. M. *Cross-Cultural Learning and Self-Growth.* New York: International Association of Schools of Social Work, 1977.

Spaulding, S., and others. *The World's Students in the United States.* New York: Praeger, 1976.

Taylor, E. *Richer by Asia.* Boston: Houghton Mifflin, 1947.

Michael J. Flack is professor of International and Intercultural Affairs at the Graduate School of Public and International Affairs, University of Pittsburgh. He is the author of Sources of Information on International Educational Activities, *as well as numerous other publications.*

Research on cross-cultural experiential learning provides some answers about the effects of that learning. Sorting out environmental and individual variables is crucial.

Measuring Adjustment and Attitude Change

Robert P. Pearson

For many people planning an experiential, cross-cultural program, there seems to be no need to validate or measure its benefits. Many who plan such programs are "true believers" and "know" that cross-cultural encounters are valuable learning experiences. After all, our folk wisdom tells us that travel is broadening, and we have met large numbers of people who tell us, sometimes very eloquently, how valuable their travel experiences have been to their personal growth. College students, inundated throughout most of their schooling by abstract knowledge, often make hyperbolic statements on their return from travel to campus, stating in no uncertain terms that they have learned more from one semester overseas than from the rest of their undergraduate careers.

It is no wonder that some planners of cross-cultural experiential learning programs do not need convincing. They usually have experienced similar kinds of learnings in their own lives and wish to make it possible for others to have similar opportunities. If curiosity about measuring what real learnings take place does occur, it is often in response to an administrative query that asks the cost-benefit ratio for such a venture.

Nonetheless, promoters of experiential learning do ask some questions — questions which acknowledge that open-minded learning takes place as a result of experience but which admit that counterproductive, ethnocentric learning can also take place. Yehuda Amir and Chana Garti put it, "It seems that interethnic contact might possibly lead to improved relations, but it might also fail to produce any effect at all. More seriously, it can even exacerbate group relations which transpire under adverse conditions" (Amir and Garti,

1977, p. 58). Leo Leonard puts it even more forcefully: "[There is a] naive belief that by merely participating in a program and being 'exposed' to a foreign culture there will be a heightened awareness and some form of increased appreciation. A number of studies cast serious doubts on this myth. With few exceptions, these studies suggest that a participant's exposure or experience in a situation do not necessarily imply increased awareness, appreciation or value change" (Leonard, 1973, p. 2). What these authors are saying is that for cross-cultural experiential learning to be effective, some attempt to design the situation is required, or the results will be hit and miss. Some persons will resist the experience and only reinforce their misconceptions and stereotypes. They may even develop an antipathy to the culture that they have experienced.

Personal and Environmental Variables

The problems inherent in planning and evaluating cross-cultural experiences are substantial. The literature on cross-cultural experiential learning is replete with information about the difficulties of defining and measuring the variables and of controlling for them well enough to assess program objectives. We can, however, conveniently sort the principal variables that influence the outcome of cross-cultural experiences into two basic categories: variables that define the individual prior to the experience and variables that are inherent in the experience itself.

Some of the variables mentioned in the literature that belong in the first category are age and sex; prior cross-cultural experience; the nature of that experience; skill level, personality structure, and language ability; ability to take initiative and deal with ambiguous situations; amount of orientation and training prior to the experience; and status within the individual's own culture.

Some of the variables that belong in the second category are length and nature of the cross-cultural experience; whether the individual travels, works, studies; the need for language acquisition in the new culture; the "strangeness" of the new culture, including the food and sanitary facilities and the sex roles; the availability of transcultural reinforcing activities that cement relationships on the basis of common interests, such as sports, chess, and the like; the political context in which the encounter takes place; the degree of value difference and world view represented by the new culture; the presence of cultural mediators or informants to help the transition process; the status of the people most frequently encountered in the new culture; the mobility available in the new culture; and the degree of cultural immersion required by the new environment.

Together, the variables in these two categories create a kind of chicken or egg dilemma when one attempts to assess the success of cross-cultural experiences. Does success depend primarily on the person who does the experiencing, or does it depend on the experience itself? Most practitioners would probably say both, but to determine the proportions in which they exert influence requires continuing investigation.

The literature is unanimous on the multifaceted nature of cross-cultural interactions. Benson states that "in general, dichotomous (that is, 'two-part') criteria have been used" in attempts to measure the success of cross-cultural ventures and that "these success-failure or healthy-ill criteria have failed to adequately describe an individual functioning in an environment, making it difficult to determine the desired target behaviors" (Benson, 1978, p. 22). On the basis of their research on intergroup contact in Israel, Amir and Garti conclude that "intergroup contact must not be regarded as a unidimensional phenomenon, to the effect that such contact has either positive or negative consequences for ethnic change or that change may be directly related to the amount of interethnic contact. Rather, contact is a complex phenomenon involving a multiplicity of dependent and independent variables. . . " (Amir and Garti, 1977, p. 58).

For those who must plan and assess cross-cultural experiential learning for U.S. students placed in intercultural settings, existing programs can serve as examples of the way in which such variables have been considered in the planning and evaluation stages, whether specific measurement of attitude and behavior change was attempted or not. For example, in an attempt to measure attitude change in their students in a cross-cultural homestay program administered by Johnston College at the University of Redlands in California, students entering the program were given the Omnibus Personality Inventory and a Community Insight Questionnaire (Baty and Dold, 1977, pp. 65–66). The results of such pretests could be used to measure the effectiveness of the homestay program. The results of this measurement will be discussed later in this chapter. In a similar study, Steinralk and Taft (1979) used a Semantic Differential instrument to assess the attitudes of Australian students toward Australia and Israel. Amir and Garti (1977) have administered authoritarian personality instruments to measure the relationship between an authoritarian personality structure and the ability to adapt in intercultural situations.

In attempting to measure the variables inherent in the cross-cultural situation itself, researchers have emphasized such things as political climate, the presence or absence of reinforcing activities, and the relative status of the interacting parties. All of these have been examined in relation to the length of the stay, the purpose of the interaction, and the degree of difference between two cultures. Leonard (1973) cites a study by Cleary (1971) that supports his own study (Hull, Leonard, and Juris, 1973) showing that students who go abroad are likely to be "propagandized" by the country they visit. This phenomenon would seem the opposite of culture shock. While Leonard suggests that such indoctrination can be prevented by systematic training prior to the experience, it may well be that "falling in love" with another point of view is a necessary step on the path that leads away from ethnocentrism.

Studies of Peace Corps volunteers in Brazil (Brein and David, 1973) seem to indicate that successful adaptation by individuals to a new cultural environment is in part a function of their being able to find reinforcing activities in the new culture. Well-adapted volunteers not only engaged in activities similar to activities, such as sports, that they enjoyed at home but often participated in strictly Brazilian activities. This finding accords with a study conducted in Israel which demonstrated that a positive attitude change toward another ethnic group was related to the individual's enjoyment of his situation (Amir and Garti, 1977, p. 58). This study of Western and Sephardic Jews in a camp setting found that Western campers who liked the camp showed positive attitude change toward their Sephardic campmates. While this conclusion may seem merely commonsense, it has great implications for the planning of cross-cultural experiences; for if positive attitude change is a goal, then the experience, be it study, travel, or work, must be enjoyable.

Pruitt's study of sub-Saharan African student adjustment to the U.S. confirms the importance of reinforcing activities in the adjustment process. She found that the students' adjustment to the U.S. correlated with their religious commitment. Pruitt suggests that there are two components to this adjustment. First, "students who maintain their religious commitment tend to come in contact with American churches and hence with some of the more comfortable features of American culture. This contributes in turn to their adjustment." Second, "we can assume that maintaining one's religious commitment . . . provides [a] sense of identity and belongingness which makes a person feel more secure" (Pruitt, 1978, pp. 103–105). It stands to reason, however, that this might not be the case in a situation where different religions were involved; there, a particular religious orientation could isolate an individual from the dominant culture.

Pruitt's study also suggests that adjustment is hindered by contact with one's fellow countrymen. According to Pruitt, Africans who spent most of their time with other Africans were less well adjusted than those who had steady contact with Americans. This finding confirms that of Kidder, who found of Western sojourners in India that they created Western ghettos (Kidder, 1977, p. 48) owing to the difficulty of adjusting to a radically different culture. Such defense mechanisms are, of course, well known to the casual observer, and program administrators need to take this into account in their planning. This author found that Peace Corps volunteers assigned alone to Libyan villages adjusted more successfully than those who had easy access to their fellow countrymen.

Pruitt also concluded that adjustment was closely related to language ability; Africans who knew English well on arrival adjusted more easily than those who needed special training in English. This ability relates to the closeness of culture criterion mentioned earlier; indeed, it can be seen as one element of such closeness. However, research needs to clarify the relative importance of language and other variables associated with closeness of culture, such as the level of economic and urban development and the political orientation of the respective cultures. In Axelrod's chapter in this volume, he discusses some of the implications of language acquisition for cross-cultural adjustment.

Research Findings

According to Benson, existing research on cross-cultural adjustment shows that the major variables influencing successful experiences are language skills, communication skills, friendliness, attitudes, interactions, reinforcing activities, socially appropriate behaviors, job performance, satisfaction, and mobility. The first four are characteristics of the individual, and the last six are related to the way in which such personality variables interact with specific environments. One implication of these conclusions is that, if we could measure the first four variables accurately and if we had some grasp of how these personality factors were likely to interact in the context of particular cross-cultural situations, we could use a combination of selection, placement, and training to increase an individual's potential for having a successful experience.

Benson also makes note of some unresolved issues. The issue most relevant to this discussion is the extent to which overseas adjustment is location specific. This is a very important question because common sense tells us that some individuals can succeed in some environments but not in others. With proper measurement tools, it should be possible to maximize each individual's chances for a successful experience, although the inability to control all the variables in the new situation precludes a perfect rate of success. Indeed, it may well be that some people learn as much or more from negative experiences as from positive ones, and it needs to be acknowledged that an initial cross-cultural experience is just one step in a long process of learning about oneself and of dealing with one's ethnocentrism.

Part of learning to deal with one's ethnocentrism and to adjust positively to new cultural situations appears to be a result of the sojourner's ability to develop a third cultural perspective. Gudykunst, Hammer, and Wiseman (1977, p. 384) hypothesize that this perspective is essentially different both from one's own cultural perspective and from that of the new culture and that it thus represents some intermediary point of view. Their hypothesized third cultural perspective consists of "open-mindedness towards new ideas and experiences, the ability to empathize with people from other cultures, accuracy in perceiving differences and similarities between the sojourner's own culture and the host culture, being nonjudgmental, being astute, noncritical observers in their own and other people's behavior, the ability to establish meaningful relationships with people in the host culture, and being less ethnocentric." Of course, many of these characteristics overlap, but perhaps the most crucial element is the ability to suspend judgment and to observe noncritically; that is, to abandon one's own ethnocentrism, which is inherently judgmental and value-laden, without artificially and automatically grasping the value system of the new culture. From a behavioral point of view, engaging in reinforcing activities in the host culture might well help to hasten the development of this kind of third-culture perspective.

In a follow-up study, Gudykunst, Hammer, and Wiseman researched student adjustment in different cultures and concluded that successful adjustment depended on three basic factors, each of which can be broken down into behavioral components. The first, the ability to deal with psychological stress, includes the abilities to deal with frustration, stress, anxiety, different political systems, pressure to conform, social alienation, financial difficulties, and interpersonal conflict. The second factor, the ability to communicate effectively, includes ability to enter into meaningful dialogue with other people, initiate interaction with a stranger, deal with communication misunderstandings, and deal effectively with different communication styles. The third factor, the ability to establish interpersonal relationships, includes the abilities to develop satisfying interpersonal relationships, understand the feelings of other people, work effectively with other people, empathize with other persons, and deal effectively with different social customs.

In a study conducted by Banks Bradley (1973), student teachers from Michigan State University who had done their student teaching in American schools in Europe received a questionnaire concerning their experience. Results indicated that most had adjusted fairly readily to their new situations, and most agreed that living with a European family was an important part of the experience. While such an evaluation approach does not allow for sophisticated assessment of attitude change, it does provide a school with important feedback on administrative arrangements. If positive attitude change is dependent on enjoyment of the experience, such feedback is necessary for on-campus planners and overseas coordinators.

In a study conducted by Hugh Brady of Michigan State University, written questionnaires and taped interviews were used to measure attitude and value changes in student teachers as a result of experiences abroad. The American students began to question their own culture. They felt that Europeans "were friendlier and more helpful than Americans would be to foreigners" and that "Europeans view the material things in life as not as important as Americans" (p. 4). Brady concluded that "the student teachers who were exposed to an overseas student teaching experience became more flexible and open-minded as a result of their overseas experience."

Baty and Dold (1977) conducted a more sophisticated study of the effects of cross-cultural experiential learning on college students from the University of the Redlands who went to live with Black American, Mexican, Chicano, and Native American families (Baty and Dold, 1977, pp. 65-66). A local person was hired to serve as a coordinator for the homestays. The two major areas of investigation were the "contact hypothesis" — "Could we detect changes as a result of cross-cultural contact which could be interpreted as a reduction of negative attitudes?" — and the "maturation hypothesis" — "Could we detect . . . that cross-cultural experiences often lead to an accelerated maturation of the individual?" Baty and Dold used five separate instruments to access the attitudinal, psychological, and physical effects of the homestay experience: the Omnibus Personality Inventory, a Community Insight Questionnaire, a Semantic Differential, a Cornell Medical Index, and a Mini-Mult, a shortened version of the MMPI (Minnesota Multiphasic Interest Inventory). As a result of their pretest and posttest assessment, Baty and Dold confirmed both hypotheses. There was "an overall increase in evaluation of the concepts *American Indians, Blacks,* and *Chicanos,*" and feelings of inadequacy tended to decrease as a result of the experience. On the whole, females seemed to benefit more from the experience, changing in the direction of greater stability and less depression. The males, relatively speaking, showed somewhat greater depression and alienation and less ability to adjust to new situations. While both males and females showed evidence of greater maturation and self-confidence, the males adjusted less readily. Whether this was due primarily to their maleness or whether the homestay situation made it easier for females to find a role needed further investigation.

Steinralk and Taft's (1979, p. 189) study of Australian students visiting Israel confirms Brady's finding that one of the major attitudinal changes resulting from an international, intercultural experience is that attitudes concerning one's native country change. Through use of a Semantic Differential and a post-tour questionnaire, Steinralk and Taft found that 92 percent of those studied had altered their views about Australia, most in the positive sense. Also, most felt that their day-to-day behavior would change as a result of the experience. While the attitude towards Israeli kibbutz life tended to be more favorable after the tour, the attitude toward Israelis was less favorable, a finding which confirms that cross-cultural experiences do not always result in positive attitude changes. Nonetheless, this may still be a positive change in the sense that if certain peoples are glamorized or positively stereotyped, a more realistic view of them may be in order.

A study of American visitors to Africa conducted by Douglas Cort and Michael King (Cort and King, 1979, pp. 211–213) used three variables to determine "some correlates of culture shock": "the sojourner's personality, including attitudes and social background; situational variables, specifically the degree of difference between a sojourner's home and the host culture; and experiential variables, primarily the extent of the sojourner's prior travel." The four tour leaders rated participants in terms of their "degree of expression of hostility towards Africans, overidentification with America and things American, and degree of withdrawal from the African culture." Tour participants also completed self-report questionnaires. The amount of prior travel experience was gauged by a questionnaire filled out in the United States, and the individual's internal-external locus of control and tolerance of ambiguity were gauged by the Rotter Internal-External Locus of Control Scale and the Budner Scale.

One interesting outcome of this study was that people who had traveled more received higher ratings on their degree of culture shock. A tentative explanation for this result can be made if age is taken into consideration. In general, the older people had traveled more, but they were also taxed more by the travel to Africa. Cort and King conclude that "this interpretation is supported by the finding that age also correlates highly with the rater's indices of culture shock" (1978, p. 221).

Another interesting outcome of this study was that people who utilized an external locus of control were not the people who experienced culture shock, while there was a correlation between low tolerance of ambiguity and culture shock. To explain this, the researchers suggested that the short duration of the tour may have sheltered participants from more intensive cross-cultural experiences. It would thus seem that both time and the purpose of the visit are important variables to consider when measuring attitude change.

Some interesting insights into the nature of attitude change as a result of cross-cultural experiences can also be gleaned from studies of changes that occurred in students from abroad who studied in the U.S. For instance, a study of Turkish students in the U.S. (Kagitcibasi, 1978, p. 141) found that such situational variables as housing for students can affect the degree to which an individual student becomes involved in host country life. The "anonymity of single-room or apartment residence in a large university can be contrasted with dormitory living at a small college." Like many other researchers, the authors of this study observe that "the sojourner's attitude toward the host country appears to change through time, the pattern of this change approaching a U-curve. This pattern represents an initial excitement, followed by more critical attitudes toward the host nation, finally resulting in more positive attitudes and reappreciation before returning home" (Kagitcibasi, 1978, p. 143). Most studies attempt to measure attitudes only at one point in time. As a result, this investigator decided to measure attitudes after the Turkish AFS students had returned to Turkey as well as before and during their stay.

In designing his study, Kagitcibasi (1978, pp. 146–149) utilized a control group and tested a variety of hypotheses, including "there will be an increase in the 'world mindedness' of the experimental group; there will be a decrease in the 'authoritarianism' of the experimental group; the experimental group will show an increase in belief in internal control of reinforcement." All three hypotheses were confirmed. The Turkish students not only showed an increase of world mindedness during their stay but demonstrated it after their return to Turkey. The decrease in authoritarianism seems to indicate that successful adjustment to a new culture demands flexibility and open-mindedness. While it is possible that authoritarian traits could prevent successful adaptation to another culture, the Turkish students in this study became more flexible as a result of their efforts to adjust.

The confirmation of the third hypothesis reinforces other studies which indicate that successful experiences bring about an increase in self-confidence and self-reliance. Kagitcibasi found that, while the Turkish students enjoyed their stay in the U.S., their admiration for the U.S. as a whole did not increase but stayed moderately positive. This finding accords with previous findings that experience of a culture does not necessarily increase positive feelings for the culture as a whole. In his post-experience follow-up study, Kagitcibasi found evidence of other changes, but, as he points out, whether these changes actually resulted from the sojourn experience or were merely attributed to the experience is not known. "Their responses reflected general humanitarian tendencies; less emphasis on social, national, and religious differences; greater tolerance and understanding of people; greater skill, ease, and initiative in interpersonal relations; greater sense of responsibility; more self-control and self-knowledge; greater objectivity and flexibility in thinking; and tolerance of different points of view. It is not clear whether these reported changes were, in fact, the result of the sojourn experience. However, the fact that the subjects *attributed* these changes to the sojourn experience is important in itself" (Kagitcibasi, 1978, p. 143).

Implications for Programming and Evaluation

What, then, are the implications of these findings for programmers and evaluators of such programs? Despite the difficulty of measuring many of these variables so as to ensure the optimum placement of students in cross-cultural settings, an understanding of what the variables are and how they interrelate should help to maximize the chances of successful cross-cultural experiences.

The first step in the process should be the clear conceptualization and delineation of objectives. For example, is the major goal of the program to have an enjoyable time, to learn something, to produce a piece of work, to change individuals' attitudes, or some combination of these? Once the goals are clear, some assessment of the individuals and the host culture environment is necessary. Perhaps a selection process to choose participants is in order. Depending on who the participants are and where they are going, some U.S. or on-location orientation and training may be necessary to promote the process of adjustment and the outcomes that are desired of the experience. In a study at the University of Massachusetts, Katz (1977, p. 77) established that racial attitudes of white people can be changed through systematic training in which white students are helped to get in touch with their own racism. While, as Katz points out, the changing of attitudes is not the same as the changing of behavior, the effects of the training conducted as part of her study show that training has potential in preparation for experiential learning. Most programs may not need such in-depth training for their participants, but training programs in general can help everyone involved get in touch with the variables that are related to success in cross-cultural placements. For example, the need and possibilities for reinforcing activities could be discussed and emphasized.

The literature on cross-cultural experiential learning suggests that on-site contact people are very useful in helping to create situations where maximum learning can take place. Such persons are in a position to help the participant understand the culture that he or she is in and to find reinforcing activities that will make the experience an enjoyable one — variables that help to promote positive attitude change. Further, such persons are able to help with evaluation of the program, whether it be a relatively simple evaluation that assesses whether the participants are happy with their experiences or a more sophisticated measurement of attitude change. In any case, some form of evaluation is crucial in order to determine whether the original objectives have been met.

While the research to date does not provide all the answers relevant to adjustment and attitude change in cross-cultural, experiential learning programs, its findings have gone a long way to explain the variables with which practitioners must work.

References

Amir, Y., and Garti, C. "Situational and Personal Influence on Attitude Change Following Ethnic Contact." *International Journal of Intercultural Relations,* 1977, *1* (2), 58–75.

Baty, R., and Dold, E. "Cross-Cultural Homestays: An Analysis of College Students' Responses After Living in an Unfamiliar Culture." *International Journal of Intercultural Relations,* 1977, *1* (1), 61–76.

Benson, P. "Measuring Cross-Cultural Adjustment: The Problem of Criteria." *International Journal of Intercultural Relations,* 1978, *2* (1), 21–37.

Bradley, B. "Overseas Follow-up Study." Paper presented at State of the Art, Second National Conference on Field Experience, Michigan State University, October 26–27, 1973.

Brady, H. "A Comparison of the Student Teaching Experience of Michigan State University Student Teachers Assigned to Overseas American Schools with that of Michigan State University Student Teachers Assigned to Public Schools in Michigan." Paper presented at State of the Art, Second National Conference on Field Experience, Michigan State University, October 26–27, 1973.

Brein, M., and David, K. H. "Intercultural Communication and the Adjustment of the Sojourner." *Psychological Bulletin*, 1971. Denver: Center for Research and Education, 1973.

Cleary, R. *Political Socialization in American Democracy*. Scranton, Penn.: Intext Educational Publishing, 1971.

Cort, D., and King, M. "Some Correlates of Culture Shock Among American Tourists in Africa." *International Journal of Intercultural Relations*, 1978, *3* (2), 221.

Gudykunst, W., Hammer, M., Wiseman, R. "Determinants of a Sojourner's Attitudinal Satisfaction: A Path Model." In B. Rubin (Ed.), *Communication Yearbook*. New Brunswick, N.J.: Transaction, Inc., 1977.

Hammer, M., Gudykunst, W., Wiseman, R. "Dimensions of Intercultural Effectiveness: An Exploratory Study." *International Journal of Intercultural Relations*, 1978, *2* (4), 384, 389.

Hull, W. F., IV, Leonard, L. P., and Jurs, S. J. *The American Undergraduate, Off-Campus and Overseas: A Study of the Educational Validity of Such Programs*. Technical Progress Report no. 3. Washington, D.C.: U.S. Office of Education, Division of Foreign Studies, Institute of International Studies, 1973.

Kagitcibasi, C. "Cross-national Encounters: Turkish Students in the U.S." *International Journal of Intercultural Relations*, 1978, *2* (2), 143, 146–149.

Katz, J. "The Effects of a Systematic Training Program on the Attitudes and Behaviors of White People." *International Journal of Intercultural Relations*, 1977, *1* (1), 77–81.

Kidder, L. "The Inadvertent Creation of a Neocolonial Culture: A Study of Western Sojourners in India." *International Journal of Intercultural Relations*, 1977, *1* (1), 48–60.

Leonard, L. *Alternatives to Lip Service: Planning and Evaluation for International Understanding*. Paper presented at State of the Art, Second National Conference on Field Experience, Michigan State University, October 26–27, 1973.

Pruitt, F. "The Adaptation of African Students to American Society." *International Journal of Intercultural Relations*, 1978, *2* (1), 103–105.

Steinralk, E., and Taft, R. "The Effect of a Planned Intercultural Experience on the Attitudes and Behavior of the Participants." *International Journal of Intercultural Relations*, 1979, *3* (2), 187–197.

Robert Pearson is assistant professor of education at Muhlenberg College in Allentown, Pennsylvania. He formerly served as regional director of the Peace Corps in Libya, has conducted research on multicultural communication, and has edited a textbook, Through Middle Eastern Eyes.

If foreign language acquisition is disconnected from the cultural life
of the foreign speech community, the learning yield is low.
Successful teaching approaches are based on
the principle of experiential learning.

Cross-Cultural Learning: The Language Connection

Joseph Axelrod

When Richard Smith was a junior in college, he spent the year studying in Germany. He went to Berlin with a small group of American students from a consortium of private colleges. The students enrolled at various Berlin *Hoch-schulen* — some at schools specializing in science, music, and theatre arts; others, like Richard, who was majoring in Germanics, at comprehensive institutions of higher learning. All the students from the consortium pursued their studies under the guidance of their program mentor, an American professor of history. Indeed, she had worked with the entire student group in an orientation workshop on her own campus for the month prior to their departure for Europe.

Richard and his elderly landlady, Frau Retzlaff, who owned an apartment building on Dürerstrasse, not too far from the University, became good friends in a few months. One evening, Richard and several of his classmates took Frau Retzlaff to see *Cabaret,* the musical based on Christopher Isherwood's *Goodbye to Berlin. Cabaret* takes place during the period when Hitler was coming to power in Germany, and, as it happens, Frau Retzlaff had lived through those "bad times." Once she had come to know Richard and his friends, she was not at all reluctant to talk with them about her memories of life in Berlin in the 1930s. As a matter of fact, the visit to the theatre that evening had been designed to get Frau Retzlaff to talk more about those years. Richard's conversations with her on this subject were part of his school work. It was an oral history project that he and his mentor had carefully planned together.

Since Frau Retzlaff knew no English, Richard had to carry on his conversations with her in German. Of course, this was true not only for the history project but also for all the little matters of household business: how much he owed her at the end of the month for telephone calls, and the like. Although Richard was a major in German language and literature, he had come to Germany with only a fair practical mastery of the language. He was not very fluent when he first arrived, and he was also very shy. Richard told us later that the first few weeks in Berlin had been very difficult; but that, as time went on, his communication skills in German increased dramatically. As a matter of fact, at the end of the year, both Richard's own evaluation of the experience abroad and his mentor's appraisal singled out the oral history project as the experience that had contributed by far the most both to Richard's knowledge and skills and to his growth as a person.

Richard Smith's Oral History Project

Richard Smith's oral history project is an excellent example of an activity that was entirely experiential and that also proved to be highly respectable academically. What accounted for this happy combination? Analysis of various aspects of the project shows that it had four features that made possible both its nontraditional character and its high academic validity.

First, the historical knowledge that Richard gained came from direct contact with an original source—a human being who had lived in Berlin during the Hitler years—rather than from secondary sources. Moreover, since Frau Retzlaff supplied only raw data, so to speak, Richard had to subject this material to his own analysis.

Second, in order to benefit from the experience, Richard had to develop more sophisticated communication skills in German than those he possessed on arrival. In this respect, the assignment was a significant challenge to him. As he was called upon to practice and improve his language skills, he had to overcome great discomfort and respond to a situation that was completely new to him. When he and his mentor planned the project, they stressed, of course, the acquisition of substantive historical knowledge as well as knowledge of methodology (how the historian works), but Richard's mentor had also emphasized the gain in linguistic skills that was bound to come—an important goal in itself, irrespective of any gain in historical knowledge. Of greatest importance in this learning experience, however, is the fact that these two different kinds of knowledge (language skills and historical knowledge) developed together. They were aspects of the same process in this experiential learning project. In a conventional, classroom-oriented learning experience, the two would have been artificially separated into two separate courses.

Third, the experience had academic credibility because it was planned and supervised by Richard's mentor, who had all the requisite credentials. It is true in one sense that the project was not supervised, for the mentor was not present at any of Richard's conversations with Frau Retzlaff. Nonetheless, Richard was scheduled to report to, and consult with, his mentor as the project proceeded, and he could, and did, modify his behavior on the basis of comments and suggestions that he received from his mentor.

Fourth, the experience yielded knowledge that could easily be placed in an area of traditional discipline. Further, the knowledge was substantive — what was gained was "knowledge" in the good, old-fashioned sense, and no justification for academic credit had to be made on any other basis. The history department at Richard's school was uncomfortable with justifications that, for example, began, "This student participated in the democratic process . . . " or even the ones that stressed methodology. In this case, Richard received credit for a course that carried the umbrella title "Special Topics in Twentieth-Century European History."

The case of Richard's special project raises some interesting questions. For example, what if another student had had a roughly similar experience that had not been planned in advance with a mentor? What if such an experience had yielded knowledge about a topic that was substantive but did not fit neatly into traditional academic categories? Or what if no foreign language mastery had been necessary? That is, suppose that Frau Retzlaff's daughter, who was away studying in England, had returned just at this time and that Richard had carried on English-language interviews with her? Would this have made the experience less valuable for a Germanics major and thus, perhaps, not worth as much academic credit? Or, to put it another way, should Richard have received double credit for his project — three units in history and three units in German? To change the focus, what if his mentor had required of Richard an experience, such as attendance at performances of the Beethoven quartets by a German chamber group that appears frequently in Columbus, that would have been just as easily available back home in Columbus, Ohio? Would we be justified in criticizing the mentor for poor curriculum planning?

A final and even more difficult question concerns the language aspects of cross-cultural experiences that do not involve a foreign language. Every year, thousands of American students have the experience of living and studying in an English-speaking community, either in the United States or abroad, that exhibits a culture or subculture that is significantly foreign to the students' previous experiences. In such situations, the English language itself, as the students experience it in their new cultural contexts, takes on certain features of a "foreign" language. Think, for example, of an upper-middle–class white student like Richard Smith spending a semester or a year at a predominantly Black college or at a school in an English-speaking community in Africa or India. To what extent should systematic learning of the "foreign" language of that community — although it is, in fact, English — be part of the student's program of study?

Cross-Cultural Settings, Foreign-Language Skills, and Experiential Learning

At a conference on foreign-language teaching that we recently attended on the campus where Richard Smith now teaches German, we had occasion to interview him about the year he spent in Berlin as an undergraduate. In the course of the interview, Richard made a number of observations about the value of his year abroad. His statement strikes directly at the central inquiry of this chapter, and it is appropriate here to outline three of his observations.

Richard's first observation concerns the relationship between the foreign culture and the foreign language in a student's education. When he first came to Germany, he said, his knowledge of the language was limited to "just the mechanics—reading, writing, listening, speaking." And, he claimed, all he knew of German culture were monuments of the "high culture" and nothing at all of the sociocultural norms of behavior that govern daily life. Moreover, he added rather forcefully, he had gained those cultural insights not through his university classes but mainly through his experiences as a roomer in Frau Retzlaff's apartment.

When we asked whether it might have been possible to achieve such insights without a knowledge of the German language, Richard's answer was terse. No, he could not, nor, he said, could anyone. For him, a knowledge of the culture and a mastery of the language had developed together during his year in Berlin, as part and parcel of the same process. However, when he was challenged to produce evidence to support this point as a generalization, Richard backed away. He admitted that he was speaking only from his own experience. Undoubtedly, he said, a student working in an English-language program in Germany could gain some valuable cultural insights, even without very much knowledge of the German language. But he remains unenthusiastic about English-language programs at study-abroad centers.

Richard's second observation describes an entirely different aspect of his Berlin-year experience. When he arrived in Germany, he said, he came with "just one mode of seeing things, one way of perceiving the universe." But his Berlin year made it possible for him to "see things in altogether different relationships, within another kind of whole." He made clear that he was not referring here to sociocultural insights but to something deeper and more encompassing, a mode of consciousness that is psycho-philosophic in nature. It is his belief that a people's language reflects, and in turn fosters, a particular mode of consciousness and that this is what we mean when we talk about someone who is able to think like a Russian or an Iranian or a Chinese.

Richard's third observation—one we believe to be of fundamental importance—has to do with students' personal development. At the time he began his year in Berlin, Richard told us, he recognized in himself a certain pattern of personality characteristics. But that pattern changed, according to his analysis, as a result of his experience abroad. He offered interesting examples that illustrated the change—some related directly to attitudes, like liberating himself from his distrust of strangers, and others related to facets of personality development, like moving away from an authoritarian personality configuration. These examples suggested that Richard was really commenting on the way in which his Berlin experience had resulted in gains that belong to the affective domain of knowledge. Gains in the cognitive domain—increased language skills, additional facts and concepts about the sociocultural norms, increased understandings about the way in which the German language works as a system—were immediately visible, but they remained on the surface, as it were, and Richard told us that he was amazed to discover how deep the other changes were. Those, the affective changes, he attributed to the experiential components of his educational program in Berlin.

In the sections that follow, we shall explore Richard's three observations as we seek answers to the central problem before us: the relationships between foreign-language study, cross-cultural learning, and experiential modes of organizing educational programs.

Knowledge of Language and Knowledge of Culture

In his study of cross-cultural communication in Colombia, Gorden (1974) found that, under some circumstances, the more fluent the American student is in the foreign language, the greater the misunderstandings between the student and the members of the foreign speech community. This was curious. How could high proficiency in language skills prove a handicap?

Part of the answer to this question may be found in the following dialogue. The reader is asked to imagine that the conversation takes place in a foreign country in the target language.

> *American Student:* And when shall I return to pick up my item
> X?
> *Employee:* Oh, Wednesday.
> *American Student:* Wednesday, the day after tomorrow.
> *Employee:* Oh, yes. Exactly.

Imagine that in the American student's home community such a response, sociolinguistically, means: "Item X may be ready for you to pick up before Wednesday, but it will certainly be here for you on Wednesday." In the foreign community, however, any native speaker understands the response to mean: "Item X will certainly not be ready before Wednesday. There is, however, a possibility that it may be ready on Wednesday, so you might be able to pick it up if you come in on that day." If the American student understands *Wednesday* literally, the situation could lead to confusion, but one would hope that the problem could be resolved in a friendly way. However, if the student has high fluency and misunderstands the response on a cultural, sociolinguistic level, the situation could lead to anger, personal conflict, and possible alienation. Clearly, if the student is fluent in the language of the host country, expectations on the part of the members of that speech community are very different from their expectations of a foreigner who obviously has little knowledge of the target language. The more fluent American runs a greater risk of conflict.

Our illustration shows, too, that where a given student group has a high level of fluency that is not supported by cultural insights, it is very likely that the curriculum of their program is deficient in one important aspect. But we can draw an even more important conclusion about the relationship between language skills and cultural insights. The academic world separates the two and regards them as distinct bodies of knowledge. However, anyone who is being trained in international studies gains more by regarding language skills and sociocultural insights as different aspects of the same body of knowledge. If educational programs planned for American students in the foreign culture do not artificially divide learnings into different subject matters, then the student's achievements in language skills and in sociocultural insights are more likely to remain in balance.

What is this balance? One way of understanding this concept is to distinguish two kinds of understanding: understanding of literal meanings—for example, the literal meaning of the word *bed* in the foreign language—and understanding of the meanings set by the sociocultural norms of the speech community in the foreign country. To obtain the second kind of understanding, it is necessary to understand the role of the bed in the lives of the individuals of the community, not just functionally—how beds are used for rest, sleep, illness, sexual activity, and other purposes—but symbolically as well.

As if this were not enough, the really acute student of the language and culture will notice certain other facts in the cultural norms about beds: Are there ways in which the subject may not be discussed? Are there times at which the subject may not be discussed? Are there people with whom the subject may not be addressed? To what degree may the subject become a matter for joking and fun?

Foreign-language teachers generally agree that the combination of language mastery and sociocultural insights can be attained only by a combination of both classroom learning and direct experience in real-life situations. But even when the student lives abroad in an academic study program, the faculty of the program may be under such pressure to keep the program academic as to give the students little opportunity for the very life experiences that are so indispensable. In some study programs, an academic-minded program director may even attempt to separate the American students from the foreign speech community, isolating students for as long as possible in the artificial atmosphere of classrooms, libraries, and museums. Under such circumstances, the students are at a great disadvantage, for they have little chance to learn the nonverbal aspects of communication, which some experts claim comprise 65 percent of the meaning of any utterance (Birchbirckler, 1977). A recently published treatise on gestural language by Montagu and Matson (1979) contains a detailed analysis of body language, with an emphasis on cross-cultural contrasts.

The preceding discussion confirms Richard Smith's first observation: The distinction between knowledge of language per se and knowledge of culture is purely academic. As soon as language mastery is demonstrated in actual life situations—not in the classroom or on artificial tests—knowledge of grammar and vocabulary, on the one hand, and knowledge of sociocultural norms, on the other, can no longer be considered separate bodies of knowledge. Yet because of the way foreign-language instruction is organized on almost all American campuses, the necessary integration cannot be achieved. In his description of patterns of foreign language instruction in America, Wolfgang Kühlwein (1973, p. 22) states flatly, "The two components of language instruction, attaining language fluency and cultural knowledge, have hardly ever been fully integrated." Many programs in cross-cultural settings, however, do not follow the conventional models for the organization of instruction. They have more freedom than their counterparts at home to create an integrative model.

We see, therefore, the central role that experiential learning can play — we are tempted to say *must play* — if acquisition of language skills and sociocultural insights are developed in balance in an educational program in a cross-cultural setting.

How Much Foreign-Language Study Is Needed for Cross-Cultural Learning?

The preceding discussion assumes that foreign-language study and cross-cultural learning belong together. Foreign-language study and cross-cultural knowledge certainly appear together frequently in descriptions of desirable education. Thus, for example, when John C. Sawhill (1980) spoke at the 1980 meeting of the American Association for Higher Education, he emphasized the importance both of foreign-language study and of cross-cultural study. "It seems to me critical that any good education . . . introduce students to cultures based on quite different value systems" (Sawhill, 1980, p. 6). One question now needs to be explored more fully: Is some mastery of the foreign language really necessary if the American student is to have a valuable cross-cultural learning experience?

If the answer is yes, then the overwhelming majority of American students should be barred from cross-cultural experiences with educational goals. The director of the Stanford University Center for Research in International Studies reported that, at the close of the last decade, only 2 percent of public high school graduates were pursuing foreign language study for three or more years (Ward, 1979). The picture is not very much better on the college level. In the late 1960s, 15 percent of all degree students were enrolled in a foreign-language course. Ten years later, the number dropped to a mere 9 percent, a 40 percent falloff. These figures suggest that there is a wide discrepancy between what educators say is desirable and the educational patterns that emerge from student transcripts. But the situation is far worse than the officially quoted statistics indicate. Fred Hechinger stated (1979, p. 44) that unless there is a rapid reversal of the trend, "the United States will be severely hampered in its international obligations." Hechinger approves the steps recommended by S. Frederick Starr in his report to the President's Commission on Foreign Language and International Studies. According to Hechinger, Starr called for federal subsidies for teacher training, fellowships for study abroad, additional funding to improve foreign-language instruction, and "the creation of some international high schools as trend-setting institutions."

These statistics leave little room for doubt about foreign-language proficiency among the nation's high school and college graduates. Moreover, even among students who have had special training in foreign language and international studies, high proficiency in foreign language is the exception, not the rule. Four well-known studies lead to this conclusion. In the first study, Carroll (1967) tested 2,700 foreign-language majors at graduation and found shockingly low levels of proficiency in all skills tested. Five years after those findings were published, data compiled in a survey of area-study programs by Lambert (1973) revealed that fewer than 10 percent of the programs on South-east Asia, South Asia, and Africa required any proficiency in foreign language. Even in the field of Latin American studies, where one might expect a language prerequisite, students who knew only English were admitted to two-thirds of the courses offered and encountered no difficulty. The third study (Blank, 1975), done under the aegis of the Council for European Studies, noted a decline in language facility among graduate students doing research in Western European studies. To complete the picture, a fourth study (American Council on Education, 1975) showed that what is true of students is true of the entire scholarly world in America. According to this report, over two-thirds of the nation's recognized international specialists are not functionally fluent in a foreign language, while 20 percent of this cadre of experts possesses no foreign-language skills whatsoever. Thus, the old image of the typical monolingual American still appears to fit the facts both at home and abroad.

Nonetheless, most American educators adhere to the principle that a full understanding of a foreign culture requires considerable mastery of its language. In many programs devoted to study of a foreign culture, especially those located abroad, an attempt is made to give the students some amount of systematic instruction in the foreign language during their stay at the study center. It is true, however, that most study-abroad programs accept students who have little or no foreign language proficiency when they arrive. Even in the case of study centers located in countries where the language is commonly taught in American colleges, such as France, Spain, and Germany, no more than two college years of language study are generally required for admission to the study-abroad program. As a consequence, most American students are not prepared to enter regular classes at a foreign university, and special programs, given either in English or in the target language, have been instituted at most study centers for American students. For example, many French universities have established special institutes for foreigners with a fairly traditional curriculum focused on language skills, literature, linguistics, and civilization (Reynolds, 1975, p. 150).

Should foreign-language proficiency be set as a requirement for acceptance to study-abroad programs? For foreign-language majors, this requirement generally exists. As majors, they begin their elementary and intermediate language courses early and will have acquired at least minimal knowledge before leaving for the study-abroad center. Of course, one of their chief reasons for going abroad is to increase their language proficiency.

Do the study-abroad programs help the foreign-language majors to accomplish this goal? It is reasonable to assume that they do, and the hard data verify this assumption. Carroll (1967) discovered that study or travel abroad, for even a brief period, had a potent effect on the student's language skills. Lambert's data also correlate highly with this finding (Thompson, 1973, p. 187). Other studies show the same results. For example, British children who went to school in France reached higher levels of achievement in French that children who did not (Burstall, 1974). A study done for the Center for Higher Education at Ohio State University (Lemke, 1974) found that the students' own description of their gains from residence abroad stressed improvement in foreign-language fluency. All these studies lead to the conclusion that the gain in proficiency is quite low when language learning experience is limited to courses on a home campus in the United States, even for foreign-language majors, but that the experience of living in the foreign speech community sharply increases these skills, especially for students majoring in the foreign language.

But the far more important questions center on students who are not majoring in the foreign language. Should they, too, be required to demonstrate some amount of language proficiency before they are admitted to a study-abroad program? Should they be expected, in addition, to attain fairly high proficiency in the language during their stay abroad? These questions are not easy to answer. If conditions were ideal, educators would not disagree on these points. The principle is set forth again and again in the literature of foreign-language teaching that a thorough understanding of the foreign culture is attainable only through high proficiency in the foreign language. But conditions are far from ideal, and some educators—even some experts in the language field—argue against a blanket language requirement for study-abroad programs. One expert in the psychology of language (Jakobovits and Gordon, 1974, p. 7) maintains that a respectable degree of what he calls "multicultural competency" can be attained even without knowledge of the foreign language. As an example, he offers American students of Oriental art studying in Japan who are able to gain significant understanding in their field even if their knowledge of Japanese is negligible. In any case, for students who have not been able to master the foreign language, a study-abroad experience is often the motivating factor for such learning. Most educators agree that the requirement for prior knowledge of the foreign language should be decided in the light of other factors, such as the goals of the program, the student's preparation in areas other than language, the relationship between the program and the student's total needs, the opportunities for studying the language abroad, the nature of the institution where the program is placed, and the particular conditions under which the student will be living. There is, quite clearly, really no one general principle that covers all cases.

Experiential Learning and Affective Outcomes

In considering the goals and outcomes of foreign-language study, it is especially important to distinguish between cognitive knowledge and affective knowledge. The profession itself has emphasized the wide variety of both kinds of outcomes to be gained from foreign-language study. There are, first of all, the basic competences—which must include the first item in the following list, usually include the second, and often include the third: (a) mastery of the mechanics that result in fluency in the four language skills—reading, listening, writing, and speaking; (b) acquisition of facts and concepts about features of the sociocultural norms of the foreign-language speech community; and (c) knowledge of facts and principles about the way the foreign language as a system works, the way the English language system works, and—to a smaller degree—the way language systems in general work.

The reader is immediately aware that these three basic competences are all cognitive outcomes. But the profession of foreign-language teaching has always stressed many affective outcomes as well. As a result of their study of foreign languages, we are told, American students will be able to accept as "natural" (or at least not to reject as peculiar) certain kinds of behavior that their peers in the target culture accept as natural. Again, we are told that we will learn from study of a given language what it means to "think like" someone from the country where that language prevails or to "empathize" with that person's way of looking at the world.

Affective growth is the most difficult of educational outcomes to identify and measure. In the eyes of many educators, however, it constitutes the most significant educational objective. Moreover, since a number of these educators believe that there is a relationship between attainment of these goals and the gains that appear as a result of experiential learning, it is crucial to know the research findings in this field.

Theoreticians and researchers in the various fields of linguistic science, for example, have presented theories and data, relevant to this question, that are highly stimulating. Many linguistic scientists believe that the world view of members of a particular speech community is largely defined by the structure of the language that they use. We often say that students of a second language are successful when they have "learned to think" in that language. Catford (1969, p. 315) avers that thinking in the foreign language means "categorizing one's experience directly in the terms laid down by the deep grammatical structure of the language." One way in which students can attain the kind of internalization that takes place when they learn to think like a Frenchman or a Finn, Catford argues (p. 316) is to "emphathize about the underlying conceptualizations," and he quotes studies done at the Center for Research on Language and Language Behavior, University of Michigan, that provide evidence supporting the role of empathy in language learning. Willis (1977, p. 75) cites other works demonstrating a positive correlation between language skills and empathy.

However, Willis also cites (p. 75) Entwistle's study of British universities, which concluded that successful language students "tended to be somewhat introverted and neurotic." This conclusion is partly contradicted by Willis' own data (p. 84). Restak, an American neurologist, has attempted to demonstrate the hypothesis (1979) that sex difference is significant, and his data show females exceeding males in language ability. Females, he claims, "read sooner, learn foreign languages more easily, and as a result, are more likely to enter occupations involving language mastery." Moreover, these behavioral differences, Restak asserts, "are based on differences in brain functioning that are biologically inherent and unlikely to be modified by cultural factors alone." Restak's conclusions, which have been quite strenuously attacked (Sterling, 1979) are based on the split-brain hypothesis. According to this hypothesis, the acquisition of what we have called language mechanics is a function of the left hemisphere of the brain, which, according to this view, processes the world in analytic, linear fashion. The right hemisphere handles insights of a nonanalytic nature, such as the immediate, gestaltic perception of sociocultural patterns in a foreign culture or intuitive perception of the way in which a language system works.

Experts in the field of applied linguistics and language pedagogy have explored this hypothesis to discover its implications for foreign-language teaching. Recent literature on the subject is voluminous; among the researchers who have done work relating the split-brain hypothesis to language learning are Bogen (1977), Gage (1977), Krashen (1978), and Rico (1979). This area of investigation may prove to be highly fruitful for educators working both with language studies and with experiential learning.

At the 1968 annual conference of the Council on International Educational Exchange, Titone (1969, p. 307) described the educative process that takes place among students who come into contact with members of a foreign speech community on a prolonged, experiential basis. He argued that there is a clear relationship between language acquisition and personality configuration and emphasized the characteristic in such students of "openness to change." Experiential learning, he maintained, leads to a clearly visible result: The learner's personality is "gradually reorganized and reshaped through an intimate, deep, and prolonged contact with the form and content of the foreign language."

The most persuasive data on this subject have been presented in a comparative study of two different kinds of residence-abroad programs. One followed an experiential model, with a supervised work-placement program in a foreign setting. The other followed a conventional nonexperiential model, in which students simply enrolled in a traditional study program at a foreign university. The research was done by Frank Willis (1977) and his associates at the Modern Languages Centre, University of Bradford. A semester of residence abroad is required of all Modern Language Centre students; each student may select either the experiential program or the conventional program. A description of the two options (Willis, 1977, pp. 3–5, 11) makes it clear that the study option is a conventional, classroom-centered university program that would accurately be characterized as nonexperiential and that the work-study option places the student in a work situation (a school, business office, or the like) that is not only experiential but also educationally credible, since it is planned and supervised by university professors.

The findings were highly significant. The work-study students showed greater improvement "in their general command of the spoken language and in their understanding of the foreign culture" (Willis, 1977, p. 30). The work-study students showed greater ability "to use language affectively in a variety of situations" (p. 36). The work-study students spent more time speaking the foreign language and less time in contact with native speakers of English (p. 54). The work-study students developed a more favorable attitude toward speaking the foreign language than students in the university program (p. 58). In terms of positive personality growth, "more significant changes" occurred in the work-study students (p. 66) and that group, in addition, "seemed to suffer less from loneliness" (p. 53).

The Keystone to Success: An Integrated Program

During the last decade, educators on almost all American campuses have recommended that projects involving experiential learning become an integral and not merely an accidental part of all students' programs. At the same time, the same campuses felt additional pressures favoring more study of languages. Recently, the powerful voice of the editor of *Harper's* has joined those of other spokesmen. Lewis Lapham (1980, p. 10) would place the study of languages and mathematics at the center of the curriculum and institute work programs as a substitute for most other subject fields. The study of languages would, of course, include the cultural monuments written in those languages, and in a similar way, the sciences would provide the texts for the study of mathematics. As for the rest of the curriculum, Lapham would delete most of it. A summer spent working in a brokerage house, he says, promotes a clearer understanding of economics than analysis of any economics text, and time spent habitually reading a Paris newspaper offers more insight into the nature of French politics than any number of hours in a classroom.

In the last analysis, however, whatever else is said about the study of foreign languages and foreign cultures, it is clear that the more integrated the total program, the more successful it is likely to be. If language training is involved, the phrase *language proficiency* must always be understood to mean achievement not only on the level of ordinary meanings but also on the level of meanings set by the sociocultural norms of the foreign speech community. In traditional language programs, the sociolinguistic aspect of language mastery is often neglected. When this occurs, an imbalance in the student's knowledge may result, and severe communication problems may ensue. Even though language proficiency and knowledge of the foreign culture are typically seen in academia as two separate bodies of knowledge, the data and concepts presented in this chapter show that it makes more sense to see language skills and sociolinguistic insights as different aspects of the same body of knowledge.

In the same way, a holistic view of the educational process sees the relationships between knowledge outcomes on the cognitive level and knowledge outcomes on the affective level, and it attempts to develop experiences that will engender learnings at both levels. The traditional model has neglected the affective outcomes on the assumption that those goals will be served by noncurricular activities. The data and concepts presented in this chapter show what an important role experiential learning plays on the affective level. The case of Richard Smith has been repeated countless times, as new undergraduates and graduate students, too, move into cross-cultural settings to gain the kind of education that they could not obtain in any other way.

References

American Council on Education. *Education for Global Independence.* Washington, D.C.: International Education Project, American Council on Education, 1975.

Birchbirckler, D. W. "Communication and Beyond." In J. K. Phillips (Ed.), *Foreign Language Connection: From the Classroom to the World.* Skokie, Ill.: National Textbook Company, 1977.

Bogen, J. E. "Some Educational Implications of Hemispheric Specialization." In M. C. Wittrock (Ed.), *The Human Brain.* Englewood Cliffs, N.J.: Prentice Hall, 1977.

Burstall, C. "Primary French in the Balance." Slough, England: National Foundation for Education Research, 1974.

Carroll, J. B. "Foreign Language Proficiency Levels Attained by Language Majors Near Graduation from College." *Foreign Language Annals,* 1967, *1* (2), 131-151.

Catford, J. C. "Learning a Language in the Field: Problems of Linguistic Relativity." *Modern Language Journal,* 1969, *53* (5), 310-317.

Gage, T. "Letting Your Right Brain Recognize What Your Left Brain Is Recalling." Paper delivered at Sociolinguistic Conference, San Francisco State University, July 11-15, 1977.

Gorden, R. L. *American Guests in Colombian Homes: A Study in Cross-Cultural Communication.* Yellow Springs, Ohio: Antioch College, 1974.

Hechinger, F. M. "Foreign Language Study: Melancholy Sight." *This World, San Francisco Chronicle,* January 21, 1979, p. 44.

Jacobovits, L. A., and Gordon, B. *The Context of Foreign Language Teaching.* Raleigh, Mass.: Newbury House, 1974.

Krashen, S. D. "On the Acquisition of Planned Discourse: Written English as a Second Dialect." Paper presented at Claremont Reading Conference, Claremont, Calif., 1978.

Kühlwein, W. "Some Social Implications of Language Study." In K. R. Jankowsky (Ed.), *Language and International Studies.* Washington, D.C.: Georgetown University Press, 1973.

Lambert, R. D. *Language and Area Studies Review.* Monograph 17. Philadelphia: The American Academy of Social and Political Science, 1973.

Lapham, L. L. "The Easy Chair." *Harpers,* 1980, *260* (1561), 8-16.

Lemke, E. A. "Role of Ability and Extroversion in Concept Attainment of Individuals Trained in Heterogeneous or Homogeneous Personality Groups." *Journal of Education Research,* 1974, *67,* 202-204.

Restak, R. "Sex Differences in the Brain." *San Francisco Chronicle,* July 4, 1979, p. AA1.

Reynolds, S. "Study-Travel Abroad." In R. C. Lafayette (Ed.), *The Culture Revolution in Foreign Language Teaching.* Skokie, Ill.: National Textbook Company, 1975.

Rico, G. L. "Metaphor, Cognition, and Clustering." Paper presented at CCCTE Curriculum Study Commission Conference, Asilomar, Calif., March 23-25, 1979.

Sawhill, J. C. "Improving General Education Curricula." An address given before the American Association for Higher Education, Chicago, March 1980.

Stephen, B. S. *Western European Studies in the United States.* New York: Council for European Studies, 1975.

Sterling, P. "Review of *The Brain: The Last Frontier* by Richard M. Restak." *New Republic,* November 24, 1979, pp. 37-40.

Thompson, R. I. "The Right to Read in Any Language?" In K. R. Jankowsky (Ed.), *Language and International Studies.* Washington, D.C.: Georgetown University Press, 1973.

Titone, R. "Guidelines for Teaching a Second Language in Its Own Environment." *Modern Language Journal,* 1969, *53* (5), 306-309.

Ward, R. "Decline in Foreign Language Study." Paper presented at 1979 annual meeting of the Western Association of Graduate Schools. Summarized in *Communicator,* Council on Graduate Schools, April 1979.

Willis, F., and others. *Residence Abroad and the Student of Modern Languages.* Bradford, West Yorkshire, England: Modern Languages Centre and Postgraduate School of Studies in Research in Education, University of Bradford, 1977.

Joseph Axelrod is professor of humanities and comparative literature at San Francisco State University. He has directed a project on language and area studies for the American Council on Education, conducted several language institutes for the U.S. Office of Education, and chaired two research projects on foreign language teacher training for the Modern Language Association.

The unique Lisle Fellowship program draws particular strength
from the way a group is transformed into a team in a
cross-cultural setting.

The Lisle Fellowship:
A Case Study

Martin J. Tillman

For forty-four years, Lisle (the name is taken from an upstate New York village) has promoted a model for experiential learning in cross-cultural settings, in the United States and thirteen other nations, that has remained distinct from traditional off-campus study abroad or cultural travel programs. The Lisle learning focuses upon human relations in an intercultural group and integrates interaction within the group with interaction within the host community. Every program attempts to broaden personal perspectives about values and attitudes in relationships between peoples of different cultures. Lisle's educational methods provide participants with the opportunity to experiment with social relations, personalize the learning of facts and receiving of information, and accept responsibility for outcomes of daily decisions reached within their group.

Although numerous avenues are open to students and other adults for travel abroad, few programs attempt consciously to focus upon moral, ethical, and religious perspectives in their itineraries. Lisle challenges participants to examine their personal values and beliefs as they move through their cross-cultural experiences. This person-centered philosophy places each individual's life experience and background against the host culture's assumptions about the meaning of life, the worth of the individual, and the values in which the ideals of progress and human development are held. Who am I and where am I going? How do I want to get there? In any Lisle group, there are always questions, there is always discussion, and there is conflict. It is a time for reflection and reconsideration of opinions, stereotypes, and beliefs, and it can be a time in which to risk new behavior or test new responses.

In the 1930s, the creation of an off-campus educational experience with multicultural, interracial, and interfaith groups was a radical idea. At that time, the foreign student community had not yet been provided with any special services on campuses around the country. (The National Association for Foreign Student Affairs was only founded in 1948.) With no television to bring the world into your living room, limited prospects for travel abroad, and no push toward interaction of foreign and American students, Lisle's approach offered a truly unique learning experience. From 1936 to 1952, Lisle sponsored intercultural programs only in the United States. The founders felt that there was an unmet need at home to increase understanding of other cultures and to expand the options of students to include practical off-campus learning experiences. The format and objectives of Lisle's overseas programs, which began in 1952 and have continued to the present, are similar to those tested in the earlier programs conducted in the United States. The following principles of educational philosophy summarize the design of the Lisle programs. They reflect an approach that as early as the 1930s confirmed experientially much later research on human relations training, group dynamics, and learning theory.

Principles

The principles upon which the programs operate today were part of the vision of Lisle's founders, DeWitt C. Baldwin and Edna A. Baldwin. These principles have remained substantially unchanged. First, there is a conscious effort to recruit participants from diverse backgrounds. Participants must only be eighteen years or older; there is no upper age limit, and thus graduate students and other interested adults are invited into the programs. Religious, racial, and ethnic diversity is especially important to ensure representation of a variety of perspectives. The intergenerational composition of the groups adds an especially fresh dimension to the learning experience.

The early groups met in a rural camp-like setting for six weeks during the summer. The site was important because it gave participants a chance to relax in an esthetic environment that removed them from the distractions of campus life. Now the types of settings have changed, but the purposes and results have not. The intensity of living cooperatively creates a dynamic framework for experiential learning. The informality of group interaction, such as in time spent performing everyday tasks of cooking and cleaning, helps to establish supportive friendships within the group. The creation of a spirited community life-style eases communications and enables many young adults, perhaps for the first time, to develop lifelong relationships with persons from other cultures, races, or ethnic backgrounds.

A second innovative component of the program was, and still is, practical field experience with service-oriented agencies and organizations in cities and towns near the home center. The larger group is broken up into small teams of three to six members. Team composition is designed to reflect the diversity of the group itself. Based on the skills and interests of participants and needs of the agency or organization, the group devises its own plan for team formation and community assignments. In order to provide a basis of comparison, the composition of the teams is changed after each assignment. Thus, in a six-week program, each participant is part of four different teams. Teams are usually in the field for five days and come back to the home center for weekends. While they are in the field, participants are usually placed in community housing by their sponsoring agency or organization. This component of the program enables participants both to give to the community through their voluntary service and also to receive a rich introduction to life-styles and values of local citizens.

Third, free time and recreational periods are interspersed with sessions in which teams and individuals evaluate their field experience and interpersonal encounters in the community and share their findings with the group. This is a critical element of the program because it allows participants to reflect analytically upon their time away from the group. In these sessions, reflections and observations of non-Americans provide invaluable insights that challenge assumptions about human relations held by Americans. Aspects of interpersonal communication, community life-styles, office routine and roles, patterns of authority and decision making, and general orientation to social service occupations and human needs in the community can serve as reference points for discussion in evaluation sessions.

Finally, the synthesis of program components and the integration of this multifaceted approach to interpersonal communication are facilitated by creative and imaginative group leadership. For most early groups, the founders exercised this blend of leadership. Later, new leaders were chosen, usually former program participants with experience in teaching and background in the fields of human relations, social psychology, social work, guidance, and counseling. In general, group leaders have been older professionals with the clear understanding of Lisle's approach to experiential learning that results from their own participation in a Lisle group when they were in college.

There is no more important ingredient to the success of a program—then as now—than good leadership. A Lisle group places special demands upon the leader or leaders because they have a twenty-four-hour responsibility. The leader is expected to be the catalyst for the duration of the program. This requires the leader to play many roles, helping participants to orient themselves to the demands of group living, counseling those who have problems in adjustment, facilitating problem solving in meetings, managing conflict and helping to resolve interpersonal tensions, and sorting out the meaning of cross-cultural experiences. Perhaps the quality of leadership desired is best stated by Carl Rogers (1977) in his discussion of a person-centered educational experience: "A leader or a person who is perceived as an authority figure in this situation is sufficiently secure within himself and in his relationship to others that he experiences an essential trust in the capacity of others to think for themselves and to learn for themselves" (p. 72).

In non-Western cultures, the Lisle model for experiential learning may need modification. For example, in the India program, Lisle has experimented with bicultural leadership—one Indian and one American. In this program, a cooperating Indian organization selects an equal number of

Indian participants to join participants from the West. The interpretation of leadership roles and norms of group behavior often reveals the different value orientations of both participants and leaders. For example, India's formal university system, based on the British model, does not emphasize autonomy and self-directed learning. Is it appropriate, then, to expose Indian students to the biases of a Western model of experiential learning? In a situation of shared leadership, whose perspective dominates the program design? Where is the common ground?

Program Design

Every overseas program requires months of planning and careful attention to logistical management. Since Lisle has no overseas offices, matters of housing, transportation, hospitality, and meetings with community leaders are arranged in cooperation with friends and local contacts in the host city. Pre-contacts in the host community for a Lisle program ensure a warm reception for the group and help to secure local support for future programs in the same locale.

The design of a six-week intercultural program is illustrated in Figure 1. The format takes the participant through the stages of what David Kolb refers to as "the learning cycle" (Gish, 1979): "Learning can be seen as a process that includes all human activity, and the ideas that can define it are equally a part of learning. Creating concepts that organize the world so it can be understood and effectively dealt with is another element. Finally, acting and experimenting allows us to test our experiences, reflections and concepts—and thereby gain additional learning" (p. 2).

Kolb identified four phases in the cycle through which persons move in the experiential learning process: concrete experience, reflective observation, abstract conceptualization, and active experimentation. They are described as follows:

> *Concrete experience* involves direct, immediate (not past) experience, the stimulation of feelings and the senses, as well as an awareness of the totality of one's environment. Someone who readily senses the mood of a group of people or responds kinesthetically to music appreciates and uses this mode of learning.
>
> *Reflective observation* involves giving attention to certain experiences and thoughtfully comparing them or creating alternative meanings. Someone who sits back and absorbs experiences and begins to

Figure 1. Format for a Six-Week Intercultural Education

Week 1	Weeks 2–5	Week 6
Entry and In-Country Set-up of Home Center	Community Field Experience	Final Evaluation; Preparation for Reentry to Home Country
	Community Resource Meetings	

make sense of them—observing them intently and reflecting on their meaning—appreciates and uses this mode of learning.

Abstract conceptualization involves creating ideas and concepts that organize experience, action, and observations. Someone who builds concepts and models to explain things and likes to learn about others' concepts and theories gets a lot out of this mode of learning.

Active experimentation involves acting out one's ideas and theories, or at least using them as guides for experimenting in the real world. Someone who gets involved with people or tries out new ideas even though they involve risk can take advantage of this mode of learning [Gish, 1979, p. 3].

In a Lisle program, participants are moved through cycles of experience, observation, conceptualization, and experimentation. In the classroom, the student, whether American or foreign, has a limited capacity to move out of the conceptual phase of the cycle. The value of the Kolb model for Lisle group leaders lies in the help that it gives in identifying the apparent preferences for learning modes of program participants. Although the design fosters opportunities to learn in all phases of the cycle, a person may show lack of skill in a particular mode. The task of the leader is to work with this individual to strengthen skills in this area. Ideally, Lisle group members can successfully complete the learning cycle during their program experiences.

The Field Experience

In the six-week overseas program, the learning cycle has three phases: entry and in-country orientation, community field experiences, and final evaluation and preparation for reentry to home country.

Week One: Entry into the Host Culture (Phase I). Ambiguity and disorientation often accompany initial entry into another culture. When the Lisle group arrives in the host culture, feelings of confusion and alienation are minimized by the support generated within the group.

Forming what might be called an intentional community, participants quickly begin to share and compare observations and debate issues in a familiar context. Housing is usually in a dormitory, rented house, pension, or other simple facility—often in a setting located away from the busy pace of an urban center. This arrangement serves as a bridge to the life of the surrounding community. It offers the group the challenge of creating its own rhythm of community life. This may be the first time that some members of the group have experienced the demands of cooperative living. The group's life-style becomes a mirror of extended family relations as they are commonly experienced in non-Western cultures. The stress and strain of competing personal and group needs require a lot of attention. Planned and spontaneous rap sessions are commonplace. Group life affords shy individuals a supportive environment in which to interact, and gregarious persons learn to reach out to include others in group activities.

The group moves to establish a daily routine in order to maintain its residence in the community. If possible and practical, the group is responsible for cooking meals when at this home center. Cleaning, shopping, and related tasks must be accomplished in a cooperative spirit. Decision making is by consensus, and the leader serves as guide and facilitator in meetings. Ample time is scheduled to review goals of the program, establish rapport within the group, and share common concerns and individual expectations.

Orientation is informally integrated into the activities of the first week. A general briefing is given to open up questions surrounding the theme of the program. The format for team field experiences in the surrounding community is examined, and the background of agencies and institutions is discussed. Team assignments, based upon needs of the agencies and skills and general interest of group members, are made during this period.

Preparation for field experience in the host culture is as specific as possible. This is one of the strengths of the Lisle approach. To help guide participants in their understanding of this element of the program design, sets of questions have proved useful. They are outlined in sheets given to participants. One such sheet is entitled "Bringing a Personal Perspective to the Field Experience." It asks the participant: Why do I want to go to my chosen site? What do I hope to learn there? Am I able to apply the ideas learned there personally? If so, to what extent and with what purpose in my own society? How does this agency/organization contribute to constructive social change in this society? What guide might this field experience provide me for future direction and work at home?

A second set of questions is entitled "Bringing Order to the Field Experience." These questions include: What are the stated goals of the agency/organization? What are the specific programs which are being carried on? How do they relate to stated goals? Are goals being achieved? If not, why? What is the nature of their decision making process? What style of leadership is in evidence? Who funds their work? What is the extent of government involvement? In what way are local people involved in their activities and projects? What appears to be the local feeling about their agency/organization and their projects? How would you describe the general atmosphere that you sense in the workplace? How did you feel when you entered — and left — the field site?

During the first week, the group also makes field trips to meet local resource persons who provide an orientation to the community and culture. Depending upon the program theme, these meetings introduce important issues and offer a backdrop to current socioeconomic and political events. Sessions may also take place at the home center, where the informal atmosphere encourages the free exchange of views.

Group life cushions the culture shock for participants and provides a secure environment for exploration of new ideas, examination of behavior, and reevaluation of values and beliefs. The impact of Lisle upon participants usually occurs in areas of what Chickering calls "vectors of development" (Chickering, 1969). Areas of social and interpersonal competence, management of emotion, autonomy and independence, development of identity, freeing of interpersonal relationships, clarification of personal or professsional interests, and development of integrity are all confronted in the daily experiences of participants during the program. Although one week is a short time, the intensity and person-centered focus of this phase of the experience is often a catalyst for growth and change in participants.

Weeks Two Through Five: Community Field Experience (Phase II). This period allows for separation and autonomy of individuals from the larger group. It is not designed as a work experience or internship. Several one-week experiences are designed to enhance a participant's understanding of social relations in the community, to improve and test communication skills, and to provide exposure to the organization of service-oriented occupations and how they work to improve the condition of people in the local community. If possible, these experiences also afford a chance to work with staff in some ongoing project.

The arrangements for field placements with community agencies and organizations involve both prior correspondence and personal site visits to ensure proper understanding of Lisle's goals and objectives and the goals and objectives of host agencies. It is essential for the team members to understand their role. We usually refer to this role as one of participant-observer. It is not a passive role but depends for its success both upon the initiative and the imagination of each team member as well as accurate perception of the real needs of the institution. Prior to the arrival of the group, a Field Experience Contract is agreed upon; this is an informal agreement between the host institution and the Lisle representative. It is important for the contract to specify as clearly as possible the level of support that will be provided for the team by the host institution and to identify the liaison person who is reponsible for the overall field experience.

The vehicle for field experience learning is the team. Usually, between two and four members of the larger group are selected for each assignment. Given that most groups comprise persons of diverse ages, nationality, and racial background, the composition of teams tries to reflect this diversity. The use of teams has proved an effective means of enriching the educational experiences of program participants. Teams enhance the development of participants' communication skills while they are away from the group. They also provide a supportive structure for problem solving and decision making and afford opportunities for more effective participation and observation within field experience situations.

An interesting recent report on the impact of field studies that concentrates on semester internships in community service agencies (Borzak and Hursh, 1979) describes changes in self-image and growth in new perspectives that resulted from field experiences by students. The authors describe how many students experience expanded self-concepts or identity as a result of their field experience.

In their short-term community experiences, Lisle team members describe similar changes. For example, participants move beyond the role of student (or parent or teacher) when they are called upon to adapt to demands and expectations of agency staff. Of course, this adaptation is made all the more necessary by the different cultural setting. Team members also find themselves taking on many new roles in their assignments. As this outcome is stated

(Borzak and Hursh, 1979), "the students [fluctuate] between postures of giving, relating, helping, doing, on the one hand, and taking, learning, objectifying, analyzing, on the other" (p. 69).

The pattern followed allows for alternation of field experiences on a weekly basis. Depending upon the length of the program, participants are placed with two to four different agencies in the host community. For example, in a group of twelve, four teams with three participants each could have between eight and sixteen community field experiences. This pattern offers a broad perspective and a basis for comparing and analyzing different aspects of community life in group evaluation sessions. As the compostion of teams changes each week, participants develop close relationships with others in the group.

The following partial account of a team field experience over a ten-day period in the Arab village of Iskal outside the city of Nazareth in Israel will serve to show such a program in operation. It is cited from the report prepared by team members upon their return to the home center:

> After these days of rest, our work with the children began. [This team had been assigned to two elementary schools in the village.] We worked for three to four hours daily. The activities of our sessions included a session of group singing where we would teach an English song and the children sang one in Arabic; small-group discussions about American history and geography using maps and pictures; pantomimed skits of different occupations; discussions about Iskal's assets and community needs along with a map of the village drawn by the children. On the final day, each child drew what peace meant to them and designed a "coat of arms" to express what the child liked and disliked about him/herself, his/her family, and the village. . . .
>
> We visited homes of villagers. The people were openly interested in our ideas and opinions on various issues and wanted to share their own views, too. We discussed the nature and purpose of our interest and volunteer work in the village; American opinions of Arabs; perspectives on the Middle East conflict in general and the particular problems of Arabs and Arab communities within Israel—especially with regard to development and improvement of the standard of living. . . .
>
> In addition to working in the school-camp situation, we traveled with our hosts, on four different occasions, to visit friends of theirs on various kibbutzim in the area. These friends had been students of our hosts in Arabic classes arranged by the kibbutzim. These visits provided a good opportunity to see Arabs and Jews interacting socially. Our impressions were that, though these meetings were infrequent, they were certainly cordial. There seemed a great deal of potential in furthering the relations between the village and the kibbutzim. . . .
>
> During our stay, we were entertained by two former mukhtars (traditional chosen village leaders). They shared with us their impressions of changes for the better in the village since the time of the British

mandate. They discussed problems of land and water for the village . . . our hosts made a particular effort to ensure that we met with a cross-section of people in the community. We met with farmers, construction workers, teachers, lawyers, and doctors. It was interesting to observe the interactions between these diverse groups and the school principals (the hosts). The principals were treated with utmost respect and hospitality, in part because they were well educated. But, more importantly, because of their role with the village children. . . .

Our stay in Iksal provided us with valuable insights into Arab culture, conflicts with Israel, and [conflicts] within the region. The program we held for the children served to give us a more legitimate role in the village.

This team report also included the following summary of key views expressed to them in formal discussions during their stay. The villagers, they found, thought that Americans thought Arabs were an inferior people; that Americans were blind supporters of the state of Israel; that Jewish towns and settlements got preferential treatment by the government for grants and development aid; and that President Sadat's visit to Jerusalem was a hopeful sign of progress for peace and the establishment of their own state, so they might have a choice as to remaining in Israel or leaving.

The team members concluded that their discussions opened a dialogue with villagers that succeeded in portraying a more varied perspective of American opinion on the Middle East conflict. In like manner, teams in this program spent an equal amount of time in contact with Israelis and compared field experiences in both sectors of life in Nazareth.

Although there is a broad final evaluation of the entire cross-cultural experience during the last week, evaluation is ongoing throughout this phase of the program. Usually, teams return on weekends to the home center, where evaluative discussions continue. These discussions become a forum in which participants assess and reflect upon their cross-cultural experiences during their field experience periods. At the home center, time is also set aside for the group to hear reports from other teams and to share accounts of personal encounters in their communities.

This process is characterized by Peterson (1979, p. 15) as "educational debriefing," a concept originated by Roger Carstensen, president of Christian College in Georgia. In the Lisle group, such debriefing sessions involve both the presentation of written reports and oral discussion. The leader serves as moderator and facilitator in these meetings. Printed forms that offer guidelines to participants for reflection upon their field experience are distributed. These forms supplement the previously mentioned sheets that suggest questions for understanding and ordering the initial entry into the field experience situation.

Week Six: Final Evaluation and Preparation for Reentry to Home Country (Phase III). The final week is less structured than the others and provides for informal sharing of experiences among participants. Field trips and recreational activities are always a part of life at the home center. In the sixth week, there is time for participants to visit friends in the community or to visit institutions that they had missed earlier.

The final evaluation is a debriefing that reviews the entire program and all the components of the learning experience and that includes an evaluation of the group leader. All evaluation sessions are based on certain assumptions about the person-centered approach of the program. These can be summarized as follows: The assessment of learning is an ongoing process and occurs throughout the program; since every participant is responsible for how he or she learns, the primary evaluator is the learner, who has the main responsibility for assessing his or her progress and development; every participant is viewed as a unique individual, and evaluation is based on the individual's performance and level of learning, not the attainment of some arbitrary or absolute goal; the purpose of evaluation is to offer supportive feedback to participants, so that learners have more accurate perceptions of both strengths and weaknesses; and the evaluation process is open and honest.

Although evaluation reports written in-country become part of the group leader's report to the Lisle office, another report is sought two to three months after participants return home. Here are a few statements written by participants after their return about their respective programs:

From an American student in India: "I have enjoyed meeting some of the most dynamic people that I have ever met in my life. And I enjoyed meeting some less dynamic and more egotistical people, too, just as you would expect in any country. I found some of the men's quiet spirituality inspiring. They sure inspired me to become more active in a public way here in the states." From a Chilean student in Denmark: "There we were, total strangers to one another and to our surroundings. What was Lisle anyway? How to start developing a joint purpose among our group members? What were the obligations of the individual to the group? Part of our problem stemmed from our different levels of commitment to the group." From a campus foreign student adviser in Israel: "I am just now realizing how great an impact this Lisle experience had on me. I believe it was the most difficult and yet rewarding adventure of my entire life. This opportunity has confirmed my intentions to make the study and understanding of this region my avocation within my career in the field of international education exchange."

In preparation for the return home of program participants, leaders also open up discussion within the group on approaches to the sharing of their cross-cultural experiences in creative ways at home, either on the campus or in the community at large. Too often, personal experiences are not widely shared by travelers returning home from abroad. Students and teachers in the program become valuable resources by what they experience overseas. Presentations to international clubs; to civic, church, and school groups; and in the college classroom are just a few of the ways for communicating about overseas experience. Such opportunities also provide participants with a chance to test new perspectives and to reevaluate the strength of new beliefs after returning home or to campus. Another vehicle for sharing is interviews with the campus press or on the radio. Sometimes, the office of career planning and placement or the international programs office on a campus will collect reports from students who have traveled abroad in order that students who are contemplating a trip can know to whom they may speak about a certain kind of cross-cultural learning experience.

Academic Credit

Since 1938, it has been possible for some students who participate in Lisle programs to arrange for academic credit from their host institutions. Lisle does not award credit but cooperates with faculty and individual students to meet institutional requirements. College students who seek credit negotiate terms agreeable with the policies in effect on their campus. Usually, a faculty member assigns readings and holds discussions with individual students prior to their departure in a program. Lisle supplies its own selected bibliography and set of readings designed to give an overview of basic issues related to a program theme. Sometimes, a student and teacher may agree to a learning contract, which outlines student goals, objectives, planned activities, and expected outcomes. It is best when all parties—faculty, student, Lisle group leader, and director—have a clear understanding of their responsibilities in ensuring the integrity of the student's academic commitments. Through a similar process, social studies secondary school teachers have been able to obtain in-service training credit from their school districts for participation in a Lisle group.

As an example of how college crediting and the Lisle experience can be compatible, we cite a recent program to Israel with the theme "Pathways Towards Peace and Reconciliation." The University of Haifa and its Center for Arab-Israeli Studies cooperated with Lisle in planning the program. The goal was "the creation of an informed and ongoing dialogue between U.S. citizens and their counterparts in the Arab world and in Israel" and "concern for the development of cross-cultural encounters that offer opportunities for the sharing of opinions and ideologies, the broadening of perspectives on the conflict, and the recognition and respect for beliefs and values holding divergent views about the Middle East conflict." Students from Earlham College, the World Issues Program at the Experiment in International Living's School for International Training, and the University of Michigan were able to arrange for credit for their participation in the program. The foreign student adviser at Indiana University was given time off to join the group because of the relevance of the program theme to his professional role on that campus, where there was a large population of Middle Eastern students.

As another example, students from Austin College and World College West were able to plan both independent study and internship experiences in relation to Lisle's intercultural program to India. The cooperating institution was the Gandhi Peace Foundation based in New Delhi. This organization collaborated with Lisle in arrangements for the program, the theme of which was "Education for Social Change." These students were able to utilize the Foundation's wide contacts and facilities throughout India in their programs of study, travel, and research during and after the Lisle experience.

A special case is the office for Experiential Programs Off Campus

(EPOC) at Gallaudet College—the only institution of higher education for the deaf in the world—in Washington, D.C. For three years, Lisle and the EPOC office have worked closely in the screening and selection of a deaf participant for the program in Arctic Alaska. A hearing student from Gallaudet's interpreting program accompanies the deaf student in what is considered a field placement for the interpreter. Both students obtain credit, and the institution has also backed its commitment to experiential education by providing financial assistance to those selected to joint the Lisle group.

It is unfortunate, however, that these examples are not as typical as, perhaps, they should be. Individual students may have success in obtaining credit for their participation in a Lisle group, but the author has found that general support for experiential learning—associated in particular with a non-institutionally based educational program—is hard to secure. This conclusion is based on visits of one day to one week between 1976 and 1980 to more than 200 colleges and universities in twenty states.

During these visits, the author interviewed students and spoke with faculty and staff. It was not uncommon for a faculty member connected with the institution's international activities or for the director of an office of international programs to become anxious or defensive in discussion of Lisle's intercultural programs. In more candid interviews, one often heard that announcement of Lisle's programs would compete with programs offered by the institution. There was resistance to sharing information about Lisle even when it was agreed that Lisle's methods and philosophy were clearly an alternative to the kind of programs sponsored by the institution.

It is also a problem on many campuses that students do not have access to complete information about options for international educational study and travel. Many institutions offer little or no advising to prospective participants in international educational programs of any kind. Frequently, the key for a student who wishes to obtain support for joining a Lisle group is a sympathetic faculty member or administrator on campus. Word as to whom a student might approach with an idea for learning off-campus travels primarily by word of mouth. It is extremely rare for an institution to have an office where both information and guidance about experiential learning are available to students. Often, there are no written criteria for the award of credit for experiential education in cross-cultural settings.

In the final analysis, in the absence of a clearly stated policy of support for experiential learning in general and for learning in cross-cultural contexts in particular, students encounter high hurdles in their quest for institutional acceptance for participation in a program like the Lisle program. In these changing times, economic uncertainty is in the mind of every graduating senior. It does seem that students are not as apt to seek out less formal avenues of study if these options are not linked to the award of credit. Therefore, it behooves the institutions to encourage students to consider off-campus learning and to actively promote a variety of programs for their consideration. Unless the student perceives that the institution is supportive of experiential educational activities, it will require an extraordinary effort and an exceptionally high degree of motivation to pursue a planned off-campus program. This would seem to narrow the prospects for participation in such endeavors to a select few students and thus to perpetuate an elitist outlook among those who do join experiential learning programs. Others will say that they would like to participate in a program like Lisle's but that they have neither the time nor the inclination to do so, because "the college doesn't award credit for this sort of thing."

The author feels strongly that students must be encouraged to plan ahead for participation in off-campus programs, in order to minimize the increased financial burden that is required. In the author's campus visits, faculty and staff would often say that students could not join Lisle because it was just too expensive. Of course, if the student stumbles upon a brochure while browsing in the career placement office in May, it is not likely that the student will be able to join a Lisle program that same summer. Yet this is what frequently happens on campuses where information and guidance is either nonexistent or haphazard. Institutions could offer seminars to introduce students to experiential learning options when they enter college, just as some institutions now offer seminars on vocational options after graduation. For students who wish to integrate both formal and nonformal learning during their four years, it makes sense for the institution to aid them in their efforts to choose the right type of experiential learning program. The personal and academic implications are too important to allow this decision-making process to occur accidentally, without regard for clearly defined learning goals.

Conclusion

As one model of experiential learning in cross-cultural settings, the Lisle approach defines a process that has great potential for effecting change and growth in people. The program asks that people be accepted and respected for who they are, not as who we would like them to be. It challenges people to live cooperatively and to struggle with the everyday tensions encountered in a unique learning community. Above all, it asks people to risk revealing themselves to others and to trust that their openness will be embraced in a caring way. Participation in a Lisle group is not easy. Sometimes, people find that they can never see the world in quite the same way after their Lisle experience. As one participant in a 1938 group has written: "Lisle played a crucial role in my search for maturity. It encouraged me to risk myself in new relationships and gave me the opportunity to test myself in new situations. Lisle was the place where I experienced the reality of a multicultural world and became forever dissatisfied with a more limited point of view."

References

Borzak, L., and Hursh, B. "Toward Cognitive Development Through Field Studies." *Journal of Higher Education,* 1979, *50* (1), 63–78.

Chickering, A. *Education and Identity.* San Francisco: Jossey-Bass, 1969.

Gish, G. "The Learning Cycle." *Synergist,* 1979, *8* (1), 18.

Peterson, V. "Measuring the Impact on the Volunteer." *Synergist,* 1979, *8* (1), 15.

Rogers, C. *On Personal Power.* New York: Delacorte Press, 1977.

Martin J. Tillman is director of the Lisle Fellowship, Inc., in Washington, D.C. He has led Lisle groups to India, the Alaskan Arctic, and in Washington.

A seasoned practitioner provides practical advice for pre-program and field activities and for post-program follow-up.

Study Abroad as Cultural Exploration

Irwin Abrams

Where can we look for better examples of experience-based learning than in study-abroad programs? Can there be a better way to begin the study of a foreign culture than experience of it? Actually, study-abroad programs have too often remained just study abroad, and the rich opportunities for experience-based intercultural learning have not been exploited. It is not that the organizers of these programs were not assiduous in arranging a variety of cross-cultural experiences for their students; rather, it is that such experiences have often been left outside the academic curriculum and labeled *extracurricular*. It is the purpose of this chapter to suggest some ways in which intercultural experience can become a vital part of intercultural study.

The objectives of intercultural learning through experience of another culture should be to gain a better understanding of the host culture, one's own culture, the culture concept itself, and one's own cultural identity and personal values. But a large segment of study abroad has always been characterized by the nearly exclusive use of traditional educational methods. In their struggle to win acceptance from less venturesome colleagues, the advocates of study abroad have been inclined to equate campus academic standards with campus teaching practices, which have often been replicated abroad. In some cases, they have gone so far as to plant little colonies on foreign soil in which professors teach the same courses, in much the same way, as back on campus.

The students in these programs, like their professors, make a distinction between the academic and the nonacademic. But theirs is different. They associate academics with books and classrooms and score them low on post-program evaluations. The most serious students work diligently to complete their class assignments so that they can sally forth on the explorations that took so many of them overseas in the first place. What they must declare to the registrar on reentering the ivy-covered portals is what they have earned in academic credit, not what they have learned. Yet their most enthusiastic reports have been of their extracurricular experiences.

How can such nonacademic experiences best be used for academic purposes? First, let me emphasize that they must be part of educational programs that possess structure and planning. We are not speaking here of that glorious Western tradition of the wandering scholar, who, to be sure, had a universal church and a universal culture in which to wander. Still less will we be referring to today's legions of young people who roam the highways and by-ways of foreign countries and come home to tell not so much of what they have learned as of the fascinating experiences that they have had. Our concern is with academic programs, yet ones that carefully nurture the spirit that prompts individual wanderings and do not thwart those wanderings with overcrowded schedules or overzealous protectiveness.

Preparation for Intercultural Learning

How, then, can we best prepare our students to be cultural explorers? Programs of pre-departure preparation have been a problem for study-abroad educators. Not only is it difficult to find the needed time in busy student schedules but the experience for which the students are preparing is so remote and different from any previous experience that many preparation programs fail to capture their complete attention. This is especially true when the preparation program provides only information about the country and does not emphasize the actual experience of encountering it.

The emphasis of the Experiment in International Living is backed up by recent research findings which show that what one learns from an off-campus experience depends not just on what happens there but on the kind of person that the student is to begin with and on what the student expects will happen to him or her. This means that preparation should include an effort to help the students to understand themselves and their motives for entering the program and that the educational objectives of the program organizers and any special purposes that they may have should be clear to all concerned. To help students to prepare for what lies ahead, some programs use exercises in which the students must perform tasks blindfolded or communicate nonverbally, thus simulating situations in which they are handicapped by lack of linguistic competence and lack of knowledge of cultural cues. We know the general pattern of the adjustment that students make abroad, and we can prepare them to expect the low period that they will experience when the early exhilaration of arrival wears off and they have to get down to the hard work of coping.

In the preparation period, the student is launched on the educational objectives of intercultural exploration. The knowledge to be acquired is knowledge of the target culture, of one's own culture, and of the differences between them. The skills are tools of cultural observation and analysis that will equip the student to be a participant-observer.

Preparation should emphasize training in the art of seeing. Cultural explorers need first of all to be aware of the spectacles with which their own culture has fitted them. There are exercises that can set them to look with new eyes upon American culture. Many programs make use of Horace Miner's essay on the Nacirema, which wittily examines certain American customs from a detached, anthropological point of view (Miner, 1956). Reading of Miner's essay can be followed by having the students read the local newspaper as if they were anthropologists from Mars or report on familiar activities in the same capacity. Cultural sensitivity can be developed through such simulations as the commercially marketed Ba-Fa-Ba-Fa or others identified in *Beyond Experience,* a publication of the Experiment in International Living (Batchelder and Warner, 1977).

To sharpen the student's perceptions, the guidelines set down by Webb and his colleagues (Webb, 1966) for unobtrusive measures of observation for observers of society can be very helpful. Without full command of a foreign language, the student will continue to be dependent for his inferences upon many mute evidences of culture. Like the Sherlock Holmes who made deductions from the proverbial cigarette ash, the cultural detective could learn to deduce hypotheses from what he or she sees on a walk around the block, noting the contents of trash cans, the pace of pedestrians, reactions to traffic signals, the spacing of houses, items displayed in store windows, and the like. Once abroad, a similar walk around the same block at the beginning and end of the sojourn, followed by recording of observations and hypotheses, could provide a basis for evaluation of the kind of cultural observer that a student has become.

A field course in community study is ideal preparation for a sojourn in another culture. The imaginative Vassar College American Culture program sought to provide students with multidisciplinary tools for community studies. It began with an examination of the Vassar campus culture and then sent student teams to nearby communities, to which they came as outsiders in the drop-off technique that has been widely used in preparation programs. In this gambit, the students are dropped off for one or two days in an unfamiliar community, with only a coin for an emergency telephone call in their pocket and with the mission of gathering key information, such as the power structure of the community.

Motivated by a desire to convey to undergraduates the excitement of discovery of another culture that they themselves had experienced in their own field work, the anthropologists Spradley and McCurdy (1972) devised an ingenious introductory course to help their students to become aware of "their own ethnocentrism as well as other people's cultural perspectives." They hit upon the idea of having the students examine relatively familiar cultures, such as those of firemen, airline stewardesses, bankers, and housewives, using the methods of ethnographic semantics, which seeks to describe a culture in its own terms. The students did not have to be skilled anthropologists to get their informants to talk about themselves or to explain their informants' pictures of the world in reports of their own. The fascinating student ethnographies published by Spradley and McCurdy in their how-to-do-it book, *The Cultural Experience,* provide abundant testimony to the success of their approach.

Another device to sharpen perception is a photography exercise. The eye of the camera is generally used by travelers to capture the picturesque in another culture or to bag still another trophy for the "I was there" collection, but the camera also has its uses in cultural exploration. Novice social observers are easily overwhelmed by the many stimuli that assault their senses in an encounter with a strange society, but if they are armed with directives for isolating and recording specific phenomena photographically, they can fix their vision and heighten their awareness in the very act of focusing the camera. In the Photographic Reconnaissance Project in the Great Lakes Colleges Association's European Term for Comparative Urban Studies, we formed student teams to photograph such urban functions as traffic control, waste disposal, and the use of open space in the different cultures that we visited. At the end of the field trip, the slides were projected in a multiprojector show for cultural comparisons. A similar project could begin with the pre-departure period.

If the student is to be a participant as well as an observer, communication skills are vital. To engage in intercultural communication, it is not enough to be able to read, write, and speak the language of the other culture; one must be able to listen and to understand communication that is not only verbal but made by facial expression, gesture, body language, and unspoken behavior of many kinds. It should be made clear that the proper goal is not just mastery of the forms of the language or even its use but understanding of its cultural meanings. Broadly stated, the students are seeking to understand and be able to use the ways in which members of the other culture communicate with one another.

Another communcation skill that students must take to the new culture is that of recording and presenting the findings of the cross-cultural exploration. The critical incident technique, adapted for field study by John Duley at Michigan State University and widely used, aids students to focus on important elements of the cultural encounter and to describe and analyze them (Duley, 1974). There are many other examples to be studied in the works of anthropologists and travel writers.

The Use of the Environment for Intercultural Learning

There is great diversity of design in the more than 1,000 academic study-abroad programs, with much variation in the degree of cross-cultural education that they exhibit. At one end of the spectrum are the programs that only slightly brush the foreign culture, such as most study tours, and at the other end are the programs that arrange for students to become participants in the host society, not just as students but as family members and workers. To ensure maximum cultural contact is not enough in itself; the payoff is maximum use of that experience for intercultural learning.

In each of the choices that a program makes for the care and feeding of its students, the relationships with the local culture are strengthened or weakened. Some programs, for example, practically quarantine their students in hotels; others place them in families or use student dormitories, with or without roommates from the local country, or they have their students find their own digs. Some programs require their students to eat together for the entire time; others use university dining facilities or student restaurants or give students a per diem allotment for food and allow them to decide where and how to use it. Even an enclave program can make use of its home away from home to bring in nationals for intercultural recreational and educational events.

In organizing a field trip, a program director may choose to use a chartered bus or to give the students their train fare and directions for reaching a meeting point in another town. Most programs use the bus for reasons of economy and efficiency, and the encapsulated group of Americans moves through the foreign landscape like Lenin in his sealed train through a Germany at war, seeing without encountering and never quite coming to understand. The alternative may have anguishing moments for the director when he counts noses at the rendezvous, but his students may also have met some local people, as often happens on trains, and had to fend for themselves outside the shelter and isolation of the group. It could even be an exercise in exploration, with students forbidden to travel together and asked to submit a journal entry after the field trip on what they had learned about the culture from conversations and observations during the train ride.

The group field trips that so many programs plan are generally of the variety that Daniel Boorstin has castigated as "prefabricated experience" (Boorstin, 1962). At the great cultural monuments abroad, student excursion groups are often indistinguishable from the flocks of tourists who obediently follow their tour guides along well-worn paths, listening to the packaged commentary and oohing and ahing at the right places.

It is far better for a student program to begin with a reading list and a lecturer and then to send the participants out on individual assignments, which are followed by a group discussion and perhaps the instructor's inspection of students' journal entries. We did something like this in an orientation program in London, giving the students one-day passes on the transportation system, and a list of assignments to complete. The only thing that gives program directors pause seems to be their lack of confidence that students can be left to their own devices in an unfamiliar environment.

In London, there are a large number of short-term programs in which the students are not enrolled in university courses and the organizers make up their own programs at their own centers. One English educator has poked fun at this species of program by asking us to "consider for a moment what might be learned of America by a group of thirty English students staying at the Holiday Inn on Wilshire Boulevard for three months" (Cox, 1978). Actually, one could hardly imagine a better vantage point from which to take cultural soundings in Southern California.

Few programs use the study center as a cultural observatory, with faculty on the staff who can help the students make cultural sense of their everyday experiences. Some programs are more imaginative, however. For example, some programs use students' journals as the basis of class discussions and instruction; evaluations; on occasion, such programs allow the records of reflection on experience to replace the conventional essay examination. A psychology professor in London placed her students as assistants in halfway houses for short periods. An education course in France arranged for students to do practice teaching at an *école maternelle,* while a course in theater had students looking at the audience as well as at the stage and considering theatergoing as an element in the life of French culture.

An excellent example of a course that makes creative use of environmental exploration was the Costa Rica program at Beloit Collge. During predeparture orientation the professor lectured on social conditions and conferred with students on the selection of field projects. On their arrival in Costa Rica, students were given assignments to locate various types of urban areas and identify social conditions through conversations with residents of these areas. In the next stage, the student groups surveyed contrasting areas using techniques that included examination of garbage cans. After six weeks, the professor flew to Costa Rica to spend two weeks with the students discussing their findings and advising them on their individual field projects. After his departure, these projects continued, finally to be brought back to campus for evaluation. Some remarkable social surveys were produced, including studies of prisons and motorcycle gangs.

The University Experience

The academic experience of greatest depth requires one to go abroad completely on one's own and to engage the foreign university on its own terms. Not many undergraduates are qualified to follow this path. The lone student must also contend with university restrictions set up to reduce nonnationals. Next are the programs arranged by American institutions in agreement with foreign universities, in which a staff member of the home school acts as a foreign student adviser in the United States. He or she counsels students on how to handle the university bureaucracy, advises about courses, and arranges for the examinations that can translate academic work into American terms. In this pattern, students are left mostly to their own resources, and the resulting cultural immersion is profound.

The more common pattern, however, is for the American institutions to arrange to have their students enroll in the foreign institutions and then to hedge them about with such aids as intensified language programs, tutors, discussion sections, and even special courses. Such programs also make provision for the grades and credits to be sent home, and there is an office or center that provides many of the support services to which American undergraduates are accustomed. Usually a faculty member of the home institution, the center director, is academic dean, dean of students, business manager, registrar, and faculty adviser and may also teach a course. If there are faculty placements, it is generally another staff member, a national, who' sees to them.

In selecting their courses, students at such centers may ease their academic burden by taking special courses about the civilization set up for foreigners, courses in the English department, or courses given by an affiliated institution, such as one that trains interpreters. However, they usually take at least one or two regular university courses in their major field as well. Professors and unversity officials tell us that they are impressed by such students.

We would note only that such American programs as these, which represent the majority of those established at foreign universities, provide a good deal less than complete academic immersion. We seem to expect much more of the students from abroad who study here as undergraduates than we do of our own students abroad.

Nevertheless, even academic immersion does not mean full immersion in the foreign culture. If it is true that *Paris, ce n'est pas la France,* it is even more true of the Sorbonne. The university represents a special culture of its own, which sets it somewhat apart from its own society. Experience there must be supplemented by a broad experience outside it. Some of this will naturally take place in the student's everyday life. Even more will occur if the program arranges for homestays or work experience. Nevertheless, while the university may be limited as the scene of cultural exploration, it does provide opportunities for cultural probing that have been quite neglected. There is, after all, an important encounter between two cultures when an American student enters the lecture hall. We cannot assume that the American students and the German students who sit side by side are hearing the same lecture.

The Homestay

The family homestay has been the major instrument used by study-abroad programs to provide students with a significant entry to the host culture and a feature of many programs since the very beginning. To Donald Watt, the founder of the Experiment in International Living, the homestay was the laboratory for the experiment. While other academic institutions that make use of the homestay generally regard it as an extracurricular asset not to be integrated with the scholarly activities of the classroom, the Experiment in International Living has placed the homestay at the center of both its academic and nonacademic programs and developed techniques to exploit it educationally in both.

Although Donald Watt conceived of the homestay as "a controlled human situation which would produce understanding and friendliness between people of different cultures in a limited period of time" (Gochenour, 1978), research has highlighted just how complicated the interactions of the homestay can be. As Gorden found in his Colombia study, for example, understanding and friendliness were not the inevitable outcomes, even when goodwill, intelligence, and fluency in foreign language were present (Gorden, 1974). The American Field Service, which has long experience in year-long youth homestays, has recently conducted important research in this area, which could help to improve homestay programs (Grove, 1980).

Because cross-cultural human interactions are especially complicated, the administration of a good homestay program is no easy matter. First, the right families have to be found, which are not the families looking mainly for room rent, while even families with the best of intentions about international understanding may have certain inflexible attitudes, such as excessive paternalism or maternalism, or they may want to take a student in order to learn to speak English. Paradoxically, the more often a good family is used, the more it becomes Americanized and less typical of its culture. Next, there are all the basic arrangements for the student's stay to be worked out, including financial matters and policies concerning responsibility and student behavior. Finally, there is the decision about placement. The better the program's leaders have come to know a student in pre-departure orientation, the sounder this decision is likely to be. There are other questions to answer, such as "Do you try to place people together who are of the same religion?" Experience indicates that it is a mistake to put nonpracticing Catholics in a devout Catholic home and that devout young people of any denomination are better received in a religious family, even a non-Christian one.

After the students have all been placed, the administrator must deal with the inevitable mismatches. It may be a rich learning experience for the student to stay with the "wrong" family, but what does this do for the program and for international understanding? How much supervision should be exercised? Some administrators check the situation only infrequently, leaving the two parties to the interaction to find their own way and intervening only in emergencies. This, of course, may make for the best learning, but there are obvious risks. Other administrators maintain continuing surveillance and are ever ready to step in to heal frictions, clear up misunderstandings, and interpret. In any case, the director of a homestay program must possess very special sensitivity and tact.

Work Experience

Work experience in another culture can provide immersion for the student that is difficult to match and that can produce an enduring effect. Work and service programs for undergraduates in this country have been much dominated and discussed, but they have usually not been designed primarily for purposes of cross-cultural learning. However, such experiences abroad have been planned with the explicit purpose of cultural immersion, and there is good evidence that their impact is significant.

When Antioch Education Abroad (AEA) was established in 1957, that institution's well-known work-study plan was exported overseas. Abroad, there could be no regular alternation of campus and job as in the on-campus program, since the students followed a diverse array of study patterns, enrolling in universities and special progams and pursuing approved individual plans. The majority of students combined study with some form of work experience, during the university vacations or at some other time during the year or more that they spent abroad. Students worked for regular salaries, for room and board, as interns, and as volunteers. They labored in factories, farms, offices, hospitals, and homes for children, senior citizens, and the handicapped and retarded. Science majors worked in laboratories and as junior members of institute staffs. Others peeled potatoes in French restaurants, received guests at the desks of Swiss hotels, served apprenticeships to Japanese potters, volunteered in work camps and on archeological digs, and cared for children as camp counselors and mothers' helpers. As in Antioch's domestic program, most placements were arranged by the college staff overseas.

On the twentieth anniversary of the inauguration of this program, we studied a sample of the 1,500 alumni who had participated in AEA during the 1960s. The most gratifying finding was that 53 percent considered their AEA experience to be "one of the most importnat experiences of my life," while another 26 percent regarded it as "a great experience." Most reported that AEA had had an important impact on their lives. The 30 percent who had not worked abroad, however, reported less impact. They were less likely to have their bachelor's degree, less likely to be able to use a foreign language, and less inclined to note an influence by AEA on their choice of graduate school and job. The profile of the AEA alumni without job experience, in fact, resembles that of the control group of non-AEA alumni more than it does the profile of AEA working students. Moreover, those who worked under AEA were almost twice as likely as the other two groups of Antioch alumni to be holding a job abroad at the time they answered the questionnaire. Those who had worked also reported having more close friends from other cultural backgrounds than those who had not. We concluded that the more cultural immersion there had been, the more intercultural influence occurred subsequently, with job immersion a major factor (Abrams, 1979).

In a companion study (Abrams and Heller, 1978), we queried German participants in an Antioch program conducted during the 1960s for foreign businessmen and engineers. The thirty-six respondents provided ample testimony on impact. Twenty said that it had been "one of the most important experiences of my life," while fifteen said that it had been "a great experience." It was clear from the answers that there had been a significant impact both on participants' careers and on their personal ways of life and outlook. They referred to a second cultural frame of reference in the United States. As one very perceptive respondent put it, "Europe–U.S. is a fascinating cybernetic model. For important private and professional questions, I always ask both my inner voices."

Antioch no longer conducts this program for foreigners, but it does continue to use work experience for its own students both at home and abroad as a basic part of its liberal arts program. Other institutions plan international experience for professional training. Utica College arranges internships in its international business program, for example, and Bethel College provides such opportunities in its international development major. Northeastern University, which has a long history of cooperative education, conducts an important two-way program. Almost a thousand international students who are studying engineering, business, and other scientific and professional fields have a job experience in their speciality. In exchange, Northeastern students in the same fields may work in Britain, France, the Federal Republic, or Colombia under the auspices of sponsoring institutions.

A good example of the use of work experience in the structured program of a liberal arts college is the Japan Program of Raymond-Callison College of the University of the Pacific. Participants study in English in a Japanese university, stay in a family, and have "internship" experiences, which include work on a farm, in a bank, and a Zen temple, and at a pottery kiln. On return to campus, they take a reentry seminar. (See Figure 1 in Michael Flack's chapter in this volume.)

The best-known program that takes students on a service assignment overseas is Goshen College's Study-Service Trimester, established in 1968 and inspired by Mennonite ideals of religious service. Students travel to a developing country for seven weeks of study, which are followed by seven weeks on a field assignment, usually in a rural clinic, school, community development program, or mission project. Small groups have gone to other countries, including Poland, and the People's Republic of China is to be added. The continuing evaluation to which Goshen has submitted this program shows that it is a program of high quality which has an important influence upon students' academic progress on campus as well as upon their values (Goshen College, 1978).

The Independent Field Project

The well-defined focus of an individual study project, if the project is well chosen, well prepared for, and resourcefully pursued, may engage a student in purposeful cross-cultural exploration more effectively than any other pedagogical device. Travel with a purpose is always more rewarding, and a particular inquiry can take the student into many nooks and crannies of an unfamiliar culture. There is a natural reason to meet people, a serious favor to ask of them, and an organizing framework within which to assemble the new observations and insights. Moreover, the student is forced to do without the security of the group and the professor and to deal directly with the culture. Most quality programs of study overseas include an independent study component of some sort, girded about with provisions for academic guidance and evaluation.

Independent study has had many meanings. All early surveys of independent study identify it with honors work, but the term has come to apply to various kinds of individual study: student research, self-directed study, study outside organized courses, and study on one's own away from campus. Common to all these modes is independent learning. In off-campus programs, independent study has been used within courses, as a course to accompany three or four classroom courses, as a major study project for each member of a group that studies the local language together, and for individual students who follow independent programs of their own. Whichever setting is used, the independent project in an intercultural program should be mainly field, not library, research. In selection of the topic, the test is whether the research could be done just as well in the campus library. In investigating the topic, the student should depend largely upon observation, interviews, and direct experience with the subject under examination.

In the European Urban Term, we combined independent study and group structure, with students taking an increasing amount of responsibility as we proceeded, until in the last three weeks — spent in London — they were completely on their own, living in digs that they had found for themselves and engaged in individual field projects. The program began with orientation in London, continued with a nine-week field trip to the Netherlands and Yugoslavia to observe cities in different social and cultural settings, and returned to

London for the independent study period. During the first weeks, the schedule was fairly tight and group-centered in order to accommodate the travel and to take advantage of local urban scholars and practitioners who spoke at planned sessions. However, there was always an opportunity for individual explorations in each city that we visited. The director held a series of conferences with individual students about the inquiry that they were to carry out during the final London period, and during the Continental field trip he arranged occasions where students, singly or in small groups, had interviews with persons whose job or expertise lay in fields of their special interest.

The greatest problem in the conferences about field projects was helping the students to translate their global interests into subjects that could be investigated in the field during three weeks in London. A student would have to be dissuaded from covering the whole subject of socialized medicine and encouraged to do a participant-observer study of a hospital experience; to study perception of the London environment with Kevin Lynch's methods by conducting a series of interviews in a London park (Lynch, 1960); to select one piece of transportation in London for examination; or to describe and analyze the journey to work of Londoners from a particular district. Such case studies proved eminently practical, and the presentation of final reports when the group reassembled at the end of the program marked a high point. In their evaluations, participants have consistently rated the field project as the most meaningful and appreciated feature of the Urban Term.

Many institutions that offer independent study for their own students abroad have left the arrangements much too loose, and the resulting study is less purposeful and creditable than programs of quality should allow. The concept is not always well understood. Many undergraduates emphasize the independence rather than the study, and their institutions fail to recognize how crucial the role of the professor as adviser and evaluator can be.

An evaluation team of the Council on International Education Exchange that looked at programs which used independent study concluded that the procedures and criteria for most programs needed to be tightened (Abrams and Heller, 1978). In urging better integration with the campus, the team recommended that one or even two professors be appointed to give advice to students before their departure and ultimately to evaluate and assign credit. The responsibilities of the academic director in the field for students' projects should be more clearly conceived. There have been instances in which projects planned on campus have had to be rigidly maintained no matter what the student found in the field, and in other instances, the communications between student and campus adviser have been tenuous, and there has been little involvement on the part of the field director. The team recommended that the initial proposal be submitted to the academic field director for counsel about feasibility, and that subsequently the director or some local expert should serve as the student's field adviser. The student should then submit a first draft to this adviser before returning home, so that the adviser can contribute to the final evaluation of the project on campus. Whether the field director also serves as the adviser or not, he or she should be responsible for coordination with the campus.

Along with other reasons, independent study on campus has been advocated because it might save faculty time. If it is to be used responsibly in off-campus programs, however, it will claim some skilled services of faculty on campus. In institutions where independent study is still not given adequate recognition in the calculation of faculty load, it is natural that there has been resistance to such recommendations as those cited above. Nevertheless, independent study of other cultures in field projects is not only a proved tool for exciting learning but an ideal instrument through which off-campus learning can be brought back to campus and integrated into the student's continuing education.

Reentry

Nothing in the whole field of cross-cultural education demands more imaginative attention than the period of reentry. Two questions must be addressed to a program on this score: What are the provisions for consolidation of learning on reentry? What are the provisions for integration with the participant's further education? Reentry is a crucial moment of high potential. At a recent professional meeting of organizers of cross-cultural programs, a hypothetical question was raised: If you had only two stateside days in a program, would you use them just before departure or at the point of reentry? Most respondents chose reentry, feeling that even in a brief workshop they could help to set the students on a course of continuing learning that might last them a lifetime.

Only academic institutions that conduct programs for their own students have this opportunity, however, and most of them seem to be more concerned with fitting the student back into the campus than with exploiting the educational possibilities of the student's experiences abroad. Many returnees feel frustrated by campus rules and regulations after their freer and more exciting life abroad. If they return as seniors, they settle in to the last months of the college grind before being liberated. Others feel that they have found themselves abroad and return with a new sense of purpose, attacking their studies with new vigor.

There are bound to be problems of readjustment. Returnees may suffer a form of reverse culture shock when they come back to something that should be familiar but that may seem so changed. They do not always realize how much they have changed. Many feel that they have had an experience that they can never manage to communicate — not that anybody is really interested in hearing about it!

It is important to encourage returning students to follow their own academic inclinations and to give them as much freedom as possible to do so. But there should also be guidance to help them consolidate their gains. A very practical and productive method of nurturing the educational process of reentry is to involve the returnees in pre-departure orientation for their successors as well as in contributions to classes where their experience can be drawn upon effectively. The real challenge is to find ways for returning students to share their experiences educationally with the campus, so that the majority of their fellow students, who do not go abroad, will have some benefit from the resources that the institution has committed to the foreign program.

What about special courses for returnees? Courses in their fields of concentration, such as advanced work in the literature or politics of the country of sojourn, are obvious opportunities for consolidation. On many campuses, students can use senior projects to pursue in depth subjects first studied abroad. General education, however, stands to profit the most. At Antioch, we used a general education senior seminar as a device for examining the experiences of a group of returnees and for comparing them both with the experiences of more seasoned travelers and with the perspectives of scholars. Possible subjects for a class of this nature range from great travel literature to social science studies of international exchange, from the movement for European unity to the cultural foreign relations of the United States.

One model for a course of this nature is being experimented with by the Foreign Studies Specialization Program and the Speech Communication Department of University College at the University of Minnesota. Part of the foreign studies minor, the course is called "Foreign Study Analysis: Transition to the U.S.A." The purpose of the course is to enable returning students to consider their own interpersonal communication in the light of an examination of the influence of their own culture, the sojourn culture, and their experience of reentry. There are some excellent readings, selected from the growing literature on intercultural communication. The students do class presentations, analyzing a particular communicative encounter in which the impact of different cultures on interpersonal communication is evident, and they write short papers on the influence of their overseas experience upon their communication and upon their potential role as social change agents. The major assignment, conceived of as a synthesis of the course, is to prepare an orientation program for a hypothetical group of American students on their return to the United States.

Conclusion

Study-abroad educators have long discussed the usefulness of formulating a set criterion for programs of quality. In my own contribution to this effort, I have elaborated a series of questions for organizers of cross-cultural programs. The questions that deal with program design will serve to summarize the recommendations made in this chapter. They have been submitted for discussion in international educational circles, where there was a feeling that they sound too much like counsel of perfection. It should be understood that they are offered here to be used like the queries in Quaker business meetings; that is, they are not to be answered with a yea or nay, but rather to serve as incentive for careful consideration of what one is doing and of how to do it better:

1. Is the structure well planned, with emphasis on experiential learning?
2. Is there provision for careful preparation of leaders, participants, and resource people?
3. How does the program lead to learning that could not be as efficiently furthered on the home campus?

4. Is there provision for maximum contact with the new social environment (as appropriate for the subject content)?
5. Is the program careful not to exploit members of the host culture?
6. Does the program further international linkages through projected continuing relationships with persons, institutions, and agencies of the host culture?
7. Is the program leadership competent in using field experience to facilitate learning?
8. Is there provision for independent academic inquiries to be undertaken by the participants that involve field observation and interaction with members of the host society?
9. How are participants encouraged to make their own discoveries about the host culture? How does the program take educational advantage of such discoveries?
10. How are participants encouraged to integrate their field experience with their reading and with the resources represented by the academic leadership?
11. Are there provisions for reflective analysis and intellectual examination of the cross-cultural experiences?
12. What are the provisions for consolidation of learning on reentry? For integration with the participant's further education?

The most critical of all these considerations have to do with the student's attitude. Learning based upon experience outside the classroom will always place a heavier responsibility upon the learner. The student who lives and learns in a foreign culture must be especially resourceful, able, and willing to venture and to dare, to endure miscommunication and maladjustment, to learn cultural lessons through trial and error. But the rewards of intercultural exploration can be great. Our student explorers may come home not only with a new world discovered but with their own world more clearly perceived and — perhaps most important of all — with a new understanding of themselves.

References

Abrams, I. "The Impact of Antioch Education Through Experience Abroad." *Alternative Higher Education*, 1979, *3*, 176–187.

Abrams, I., and Heller, F. "Evaluating Academic Programs Abroad: The CIEE Project." *CIEE Occasional Papers*, no. 21. New York: Council for International Education Exchange, 1978.

Batchelder, D., and Warner, E. G. *Beyond Experience*. Brattleboro, Vt.: Experiment Press, 1977.

Boorstin, D. J. *The Image*. New York: Atheneum, 1962.

Cox, E. H. "Great Britain." In B. B. Burn (Ed.), *Higher Education Reform: Implications for Foreign Students*. New York: Institute of International Education, 1978.

Duley, J. "Cross-Cultural Field Study." In J. Duley (Ed.), *New Directions for Higher Education: Implementing Field Experience Education*, no. 6. San Francisco: Jossey-Bass, 1974.

Gochenour, T. "The Homestay." *Odysses International, the Publication of the Experiment and Its School for International Training*, 1978, *1* (3), 7.

Gorden, R. L. *American Guests in Colombian Homes: A Study in Cross-Cultural Communication*. Yellow Springs, Ohio: Antioch College, 1974.

Goshen College. *Goshen College SST: A Concise Summary.* Goshen, Ind.: Goshen College, 1978.

Grove, N. *The AFS Family Characteristics and Impact Studies: A Report of the Findings.* New York: American Field Service, 1980.

Lynch, K. *The Image of the City.* Cambridge, Mass.: M.I.T. Press, 1960.

Miner, H. "Body Ritual Among the Nacirema." *American Anthropologist,* 1956, *56,* 503–507.

Spradley, J. P., and McCurdy, D. W. *The Cultural Experience.* Palo Alto, Calif.: Science Research Associates, 1972.

*Irwin Abrams is Distinguished University Professor, Antioch University.
As professor of history at Antioch College, he helped establish
Antioch Education Abroad in 1957 and has published widely on study
abroad. As coordinator of International Programs of the Great Lakes
Colleges Association, he developed the GLCA European Term on
Comparative Studies.*

The observations of the preceding chapters are considered
and suggestions offered for strengthening support
for cross-cultural learning.

Some Concluding Observations and Further Resources

Charles B. Neff

The preceding chapters have addressed theory, research, and student learning and examined some practical questions related to cross-cultural experiential education. These contributions and many others in the literature are all part of a substantial agenda for promoting and expanding—or, in times of fiscal austerity, for protecting and maintaining—experiential learning in other cultures. This agenda consists of the following major areas.

Building Commitment: A Primary Issue

Overriding such specific issues as organization, design, assessment, and reward, which will all be discussed later, there is a general strategic issue that must be addressed by all the constituencies involved—campus, consortial, and governmental. Without confronting it at the outset, we are unlikely to deal with the additional issues effectively. That overriding general issue is how to forge a commitment for cross-cultural experiential education. I would maintain that, if it is going to of any lasting value, such a commitment will consist of two distinct elements: promotion of the educational value of cross-cultural experiential learning in its own right and recognition that education about international affairs and involvement with the world is in the national interest. These two aspects of the issue of commitment fit very closely together.

Promotion of the educational merit of cross-cultural experiential learning will occur only through an active coalition of campus and consortial groups. Initially, campuses that have strong intercultural learning programs will need to protect them as much as possible against the eroding forces of rising costs and inflation. Thereafter, there should be some movement toward expansion and development. It is encouraging that the number of students who have enrolled in study-abroad programs has remained relatively constant over the last five years, as confirmed by IIE statistics. However, at least one analyst feels that sharply rising travel costs and the costs of living abroad have not yet begun to have serious effects upon study-abroad enrollments, although they very well may have an effect in the near future (James, 1980). In the State University of New York, which operates the largest number of study-abroad programs of any university in the United States, seventy-seven in all, a similar concern has been expressed by a number of campus administrators.

Luckily, some colleges have deliberately, in the last few years, done more than to protect study-abroad programs; they have invested heavily in them, making them a central part of their curricular offerings. St. Olaf College not only offers a variety of locations in which students can study but also has developed four different styles of programs: interim abroad, Far East term, independent study, and service learning (James, 1980). Lewis and Clark College has developed a unique method for linking overseas study programs with an ambitiously designed cross-cultural general studies program for freshmen (Thompson, 1980).

But more will be needed than just the efforts of individual campuses. Some of the organizations that have strong interests in international programs, such as the National Association for Foreign Student Affairs, the Institute of International Education, the Council on International Educational Exchange, the Experiment for International Living, the Lisle Fellowship, and Crossroad Africa, may have to band together with the Council for the Advancement of Experiential Learning (CAEL) to mount a national demonstration program designed both to call attention to experiential cross-cultural learning and to develop new forms for it. With foundation and federal support, the international/CAEL effort could conduct research on existing experiential cross-cultural learning programs as well as design, plan, and implement experimental programs drawing personnel and students from several campuses and organizations. The experimentation could be both in program design (how much classroom teaching, student support, and post-experience emphasis) and in location. The effort might purposefully emphasize study and experience in parts of the developing world where cross-cultural experiences have been limited. As a capstone of the effort, the experiments could be thoroughly assessed and the results of the assessment returned to the campuses in an effort to encourage further experimentation in campus programs.

Parallel to an effort putting the spotlight on new forms of cross-cultural experiential learning and the proper means for assessing them, the same campus consortial and associational groups need also to assist in the formation of a more effective national constituency to lobby in the Congress, the executive branch, and state legislatures for funding to help defray the costs of study abroad for individual students, to encourage foreign-language in-area studies, and to provide experimental funding for cross-cultural learning programs.

There is much support for the development of precisely that kind of constituency in the report of the President's Commission on Foreign Language and International Studies (1979). This report advocates the position that cross-cultural learning is of national concern. In its covering letter, the Commission trenchantly links language and area studies to the national interest: "The hard and brutal fact is that our programs in institutions for education and training for foreign language and international understanding are both currently inadequate and actually falling further behind. This growing deficiency must be corrected if we are to secure our national objectives as we enter the twenty-first century" (1979, p. 1).

The Commission notes that only 15 percent of American high school students now study a foreign language; only 8 percent of American colleges and universities now require foreign language for admission; foreign affairs agencies of the U.S. government are deeply concerned that declining foreign-language enrollments in our schools and colleges will lower the quality of new recruits for their services. Between 1967 and 1980, the Ford Foundation reduced its contribution to the support of area studies sevenfold, and by 1978 the Fulbright exchange program had effectively been cut to one-third of its level in 1969. The Commission makes many recommendations that could form the basis for action by a national constituency.

A private citizens group, the National Council on Foreign Language and International Studies, has now been established to carry out some of the recommendations of the President's Commission. But there is a danger. If this group draws primarily from the Commission report, its focus may be on the traditional classroom issues of language and area-study instruction. While attention to such issues is certainly necessary, one may hope that it will not lead to exclusion of the important educational perspectives represented by experiential cross-cultural learning programs. That is why the first part of the commitment—to the experiential learning programs themselves—is necessary. Demonstration of the importance of cross-cultural experiential learning must be considered an important part of a national effort, not a curiosity or a frill.

Organizational Issues

The question of how best to build a national coalition that pays attention to experiential cross-cultural education as well as to other matters has its analog in organizational issues on the campus. For instance, what are the advantages and disadvantages of placing the responsibility for operation of cross-cultural and experiential learning programs in a separate office or in a study-abroad office? In an office that has responsibility for all experiential learning programs or in the separate departments? A separate organization for experiential cross-cultural learning might allow and even encourage more experimentation than if the experience were filtered through traditional academic forms. Separatism, however, runs immediately up against the question of financing. All programs cost more these days, and perhaps the worst thing that could be done for experimental programs is to put them in direct competition for resources with academic departments. Further, distance from the recognized sources of academic legitimacy makes it difficult to credit the experience and can create another either/or choice: either the experience or the credit.

It seems that the best overall answer would be a compromise whereby some of the responsibility would be borne by an office independent of the academic departments but the overall design of the experience would result in some integration of the experimental with the traditional. Departments certainly need to be brought in on any pre-experience learning, for they will continue to teach most of the courses that students will need in order to prepare themselves for a cross-cultural experience. Departments should provide advice in the designing of assessment of the academic value of the experience because, for the most part, they will have the responsibility for rewarding that experience with traditional academic credits.

I would maintain, however, that probably the most promising route for the integration of traditional and experiential approaches is increased attention to the place of experiential cross-cultural education in the general education curriculum. While not always true, it is usually the case that the more advanced the level at which a discipline is being studied, the more difficult it is to bring interdisciplinary, much less educational and experiential, perspectives into the curriculum. The general education curriculum is more suitable for looking at topics in breadth, rather than in depth, a characteristic that is important to cross-cultural education. The loosely organized general education curriculum allows more possibilities for the incorporation of experiential learning into its design than the disciplinary programs, with the possible exception of professional programs.

General education curricula are currently being reexamined after the damage done to them by the academic anarchy of the 1960s. It is, therefore, a propitious time to raise the very important issue of whether some kind of cross-cultural emphasis, whether experiential or not, should be included or even required of every student in the redesigned offerings (Cleveland, 1980). Most programs will probably not accept such an emphasis as a requirement, but it is not unreasonable to insist that every general education curriculum should include a visible and attractive cross-cultural education option, and, if at all possible, that option should also include an opportunity for some of the learning to occur through direct experience of another culture.

Of course, there is no need to make a strict or limiting distinction between general education and advanced education either in the area of cross-cultural learning or in any other. Just as the organizational issue of how to operate cross-cultural experiential learning programs will probably be settled in most cases by compromise, so will the way of relating general education to specialized education best be settled by collaboration. The ideal situation will probably be one in which students are given an opportunity to learn broadly about other cultures early in their education, to have some kind of direct experience of the culture, and to study the more complex parts of that culture in depth on the home campus within the context of a discipline. In this way, students could relate their specialized knowledge to the experience that they have acquired.

Design Issues

Certain good program characteristics of cross-cultural experiential learning should be preserved regardless of the precise model employed. For instance, there is unanimous agreement among our contributors, and others who have operated programs, about the necessity for good pre-program orientation and preparation. There is substantial agreement that people need assistance in working their way back into home campus programs, particularly if they have been away for a long time or they have been in largely unstructured situations. There is not very much agreement about the level of support services that should be available to students while they are living in another culture. Some persons maintain that the experience is enhanced to the degree that students are left on their own. Others argue that younger students in particular do not have the self-discipline or motivation to make full use of their experience and that fairly close monitoring by support staff is required to reach the goal.

Perhaps comparative studies on the effects of different types of support services in the field are needed. The junior year abroad model has served us well, yet it may not be the best type of program for all students. In its most usual form, it keeps students together as a group and often inhibits extensive contact with the host culture. This is especially true to the extent that the faculty who teach the students are transplanted Americans. There are probably other models that may better serve different types of students. Just as students on the home campus can be divided into students who thrive best in structured situations and students who can be generally self-directive, we can presume the same will be true of students in cross-cultural experiential learning situations. Matching the program design to the types of students and to their learning styles would seem to increase the possibility of success. (Pearson's chapter in this volume supports that view.) The variety of options offered by St. Olaf College, which has programs ranging from short-term to long-term and from closely monitored to highly individualistic, would seem to be a good approach (James, 1980).

Two other design issues also deserve attention. Most study-abroad programs continue to be in Western Europe or in cultures that are relatively familiar to Americans (Boyan and others, 1980, p. 73). Programs in Third-World countries have been very difficult to establish for a variety of reasons — lack of housing, extreme distance between home and host cultures, political instability, high costs, and so forth. But that part of the world is growing rapidly, and there is every likelihood that its contacts with the industrialized West will increase. Certainly, it ought to be part of our thinking that more attention should be given to establishment of programs in Third-World countries, regardless of the initial difficulties.

Finally, the same question of balance could be extended to a comparison of the range of programs available abroad to the programs available in subcultural areas in the United States. It is not clear that the existing balance between cross-cultural experience in foreign countries and in domestic settings is the best. As we think of protecting and even expanding cross-cultural study abroad, we should also be giving some attention to experiments with programs for Americans within the subcultures of their own country. At least one study maintains that experience in a foreign culture does not produce any more learning than contact with a national subculture close to home (Hull, Lemke, and Houang, 1977).

Assessment Issues

A good deal of work has already been done to determine the effects of cross-cultural experiential learning. Nevertheless, there seems to be a need for more work in areas that show great promise but are not fully developed. For instance, little work has been done on the assessment of empathy, understanding, and personal growth, all of which are often cited as important desired outcomes.

Through a variety of research and program efforts sponsored by the Council for the Advancement of Experiential Learning, a great deal of progress on the assessment of both college-sponsored and nonsponsored or "prior" experiential learning has been made. Program administrators in study-abroad programs should find the results of these efforts useful in dealing with the assessment of experiential learning in cross-cultural settings. (A list of relevant publications is available from CAEL, 300 Lakefront North, Columbia, Maryland 21044.)

Reward Issues

Reward issues fall into two major categories: rewards for faculty and rewards for students. The situation of persons working in cross-cultural experiential learning is the same as the one that faces faculty when they are engaged in any kind of innovative program. Is the work that they are doing considered good enough as teaching or research to meet the professional standards of excellence established by their colleagues through the departments and disciplines? This issue will continue to be fought out in a variety of ways. There is no substitute for a campus administration to say at the outset and in unequivocal terms that experiential learning is a legitimate form of education. The people who participate in experiential programs should not be penalized; it is to be preferred, however, that they will be rewarded in ways that are manifestly equitable. It is encouraging that in some schools, such as Occidental College, St. Olaf College, and Lewis and Clark College, that the programs themselves require large numbers of faculty to become involved in cross-cultural experiential learning programs, not necessarily in the same year but over time (James, 1980; Speich, 1980; Thompson, 1980). If involvement with experiential learning becomes a common experience for large numbers of faculty, the issue of whether faculty should be rewarded for such activity may fade of its own accord.

Rewards for students are involved in the same issues, but they take a different form. Should students be rewarded only for the part of their experience that is equivalent to a normal academic practice? Should cross-cultural education be judged by its resemblance to on-campus instruction? If other parts of the experience, such as changes in empathy, commitment, and development, are recognized, how are they to be rewarded?

By and large, the currency of academic reward is the credits granted toward graduation. As long as those credits are defined according to traditional standards, there is a very good chance that only those activities which resemble traditional academic instruction will receive the necessary recognition. However, as the total curriculum begins to include experiential learning, some of the difficulty encountered in crediting experiential learning in the past may disappear. One may hope that this will occur. (For a discussion of some of the problems involving credit for experiential learning, see Martorana and Kuhns, 1979.)

Final Comments

A recent article titled "What Students Should Know About Their World" (Barrows, Clark, and Klein, 1980) provides some insights into why we should be concerned about the future of cross-cultural experiential learning. First, the authors confirm the general findings of the President's Commission on Foreign Language and International Studies: Americans possess partial and distorted information about affairs in the world around them. Specifically, 1,000 college seniors achieved a mean score of 50.5 questions correct on a 101-item test, which shows a considerable lack of knowledge on topics felt by the assessment committee to be important. In addition, even the able students had misconceptions about such things as nutrition, human rights, oil politics, and patterns of world birthrates and deathrates.

The same authors report on what they call "a psychological view of global understanding." Three separate components emerged from their analysis of twenty-one variables. One component dealt with knowledge, one with foreign language, and a third with affect. *High knowledge* meant a high score on a global understanding test, making a rule of reading international news, a low score on a chauvinism scale, and a high score on a concern scale and a human rights scale. *High foreign language* meant high scores in speaking, listening, and reading ability, time in foreign areas, and attitudes toward foreign language learning and a relatively high score on the concern scale. *Affect or attitude* was measured by a number of attitudinal variables: "'left' [that is, liberal] political orientation would appear to be associated with concerned, cooperative, pro-world government, pro-human rights, antiwar, and antichauvinistic sentiments."

The authors found a clear distinction and absence of overlap between knowledge and language factors. Affect, however, seemed to overlap moderately with knowledge and to a lesser extent with language as well. Although the correlations are low and the data will be reanalyzed, it already seems that the affective variables, which many proponents of cross-cultural experiential learning think are desirable, mediate between knowledge about the world and ability to use a foreign language. Whether these attitudes encourage the understanding of language or whether the knowledge of language affects these attitudes, whether it is knowledge that changes attitudes or attitudes that encourage the acquisition of knowledge, we do not know. Answers may emerge from further analysis.

It is fascinating, however, that it is possible to know a language and not know very much about the world or to be well informed about the world without ever having studied a foreign language. What brings language and knowledge together are attitudes that research generally, though not invariably, shows to be positively developed through contact with foreign cultures.

In other words, we could profitably mount a national effort to increase knowledge or to increase enrollments in foreign languages. But without the intervening effect of attitudinal change brought about through experience, the goal of providing a full international education for a significantly larger portion of our population is not likely to be realized. Knowledge, yes; foreign-language training, yes; but experience, too. That is why the expansion and enhancement of cross-cultural learning is vitally important.

Additional Resources/Organizations

The following list of organizations excludes those that are involved exclusively or primarily in the operation of study-abroad programs. The organizations included in the following list may operate such programs, but additionally publish, regularly or periodically, materials useful in understanding the nature of cross-cultural experiential education.

1. American Field Service, 313 East 43rd Street, New York, New York 10017.

   AFS has a research division which produces occasional publications. Of particular note is *The AFS Family Characteristics and Impact Studies: A Report of the Findings.* September, 1980.

2. Council on International Education Exchange, 205 East 42nd Street, New York, New York 10017.

   CIEE produces a number of regular publications, several dealing with study abroad in Europe, Italy, France, Great Britain, Ireland, Asia, and Latin America. Of particular interest is *The Whole World Handbook*, which is updated annually. CIEE also has a series of occasional papers that deal with particular research topics.

3. Institute of International Education, Communications Division, 809 United Nations Plaza, New York, New York 10017.

   IIE produces a number of research reports, principally its annual report on the international exchanges of persons, *Open Doors*. It also publishes the *World Higher Education Communiqué*, a quarterly journal offering a global perspective on trends, issues, and news events that could impact on international educational exchange.

4. International Communications Agency, Office of Congressional and Public Liaison, Room 106, 1750 Pennsylvania Avenue NW, Washington, D.C. 20547.

ICA publishes a *Directory of Resources for Cultural and Educational Exchanges and International Communication.* Further information about this publication is available through the ICA Training Division and the Office of Research.

5. International Society for Education, Cultural, and Scientific Interchanges, Antioch International, Yellow Springs, Ohio 45387.

   ISECSI publishes a *Bulletin of International Interchanges.*

6. Interversitas, Northeastern University, 5500 North St. Louis Avenue, Chicago, Illinois 60625.

   Interversitas is a relatively new organization with international membership; publishes a *Newsletter of Interversitas,* which provides information on individual association members, their current activities and research interests.

7. National Association for Foreign Student Affairs, 1860 19th Street NW, Washington, D.C. 20009.

   Although NAFSA is primarily concerned with foreign students in the United States, it also publishes occasional papers dealing with cultural education involving Americans abroad, for instance, the *Study Abroad Handbook for Advisors and Administrators,* 1979.

8. Society for Intercultural Educational Training and Research, c/o Dr. Paul Pederson, Georgetown University, Washington, D.C. 20057.

   SIETR publishes *The International Journal of Intercultural Relations.*

References

Barrows, T., Clark, J., and Klein, S. "What Students Know About Their World." *Change,* 1980, *12* (4), 10–17.

Boyan, D. R., and Julian, A. C. (Eds.). *Open Doors: 1978–79.* New York: Institute of International Education, 1980.

Cleveland, H. "Forward to Basics." *Change,* 1980, *12* (4), 18–22.

Duley, J. (Ed.). *New Directions for Higher Education: Implementing Field Experience Education,* no. 6. San Francisco: Jossey-Bass, 1974.

Hull, W. F., IV, Lemke, H., Jr., and Houang, R. T. *The American Undergraduate, Off-Campus and Overseas: A Study of the Educational Validity of Such Programs.* New York: Council on International Educational Exchange, 1977.

James, N. A. "The Faraway Classroom." *Change,* 1980, *12* (4), 58–59.

Martorana, S. V., and Kuhns, E. (Eds.). *New Directions for Experiential Learning: Transferring Experiential Credit,* no. 4. San Francisco: Jossey-Bass, 1979.

The President's Commission on Foreign Language and International Studies. *Strength Through Wisdom: A Critique of U.S. Capability.* Washington, D.C.: U.S. Government Printing Office, 1979.

Speich, D. F. "A Long History of Global Emphasis." *Change,* 1980, *12* (4), 65–67.

Thompson, W. "Equal Opportunity Internationalism." *Change,* 1980, *12* (4), 64–65.

Charles B. Neff was formerly associate vice-chancellor for international programs of the State University of New York. He also served as director of Educational Programs for the Peace Corps in Colombia and was for thirteen years at the University of Hawaii. He is currently president of the Associated Colleges of the Midwest (A.C.M.), in Chicago.

Index

New Directions Quarterly Sourcebooks

New Directions for Experiential Learning is one of several distinct series of quarterly sourcebooks published by Jossey-Bass. The sourcebooks in each series are designed to serve both as *convenient compendiums* of the latest knowledge and practical experience on their topics and as *long-life reference tools.*

One-year, four-sourcebook subscriptions for each series cost $18 for individuals (when paid by personal check) and $30 for institutions, libraries, and agencies. Single copies of earlier sourcebooks are available at $6.95 each *prepaid* (or $7.95 each when *billed*).

A complete listing is given below of current and past sourcebooks in the *New Directions for Experiential Learning* series. The titles and editors-in-chief of the other series are also listed. To subscribe, or to receive further information, write: New Directions Subscriptions, Jossey-Bass Inc., Publishers, 433 California Street, San Francisco, California 94104.

New Directions for Experiential Learning
Pamela J. Tate, Editor-in-Chief
Morris T. Keeton, Consulting Editor
1978–1979: 1. *Learning by Experience — What, Why, How,*
                Morris T. Keeton, Pamela J. Tate
            2. *Developing and Expanding Cooperative Education,*
                James W. Wilson
            3. *Defining and Measuring Competence,*
                Paul S. Pottinger, Joan Goldsmith
            4. *Transferring Experiential Credit,* S. V. Martorana,
                Eileen Kuhns
1979–1980: 5. *Combining Career Development with Experiential Learning,*
                Frank D. van Aalst
            6. *Enriching the Liberal Arts Through Experiential Learning,*
                Stevens Brooks, James Althof
            7. *Developing New Adult Clienteles by Recognizing Prior
                Learning,* Rexford G. Moon, Gene R. Hawes
            8. *Developing Experiential Learning Programs for Professional
                Education,* Eugene T. Byrne, Douglas E. Wolfe
1980–1981: 9. *Defining and Assuring Quality in Experiential Learning,*
                Morris T. Keeton
           10. *Building New Alliances: Labor Unions and Higher
                Education,* Hal Stack, Carroll M. Hutton

New Directions for Child Development
William Damon, Editor-in-Chief

New Directions for College Learning Assistance
Kurt V. Lauridsen, Editor-in-Chief

New Directions for Community Colleges
Arthur M. Cohen, Editor-in-Chief
Florence B. Brawer, Associate Editor

New Directions for Continuing Education
Alan B. Knox, Editor-in-Chief

New Directions for Exceptional Children
James J. Gallagher, Editor-in-Chief

New Directions for Higher Education
JB Lon Hefferlin, Editor-in-Chief

New Directions for Institutional Advancement
A. Westley Rowland, Editor-in-Chief

New Directions for Institutional Research
Marvin W. Peterson, Editor-in-Chief

New Directions for Mental Health Services
H. Richard Lamb, Editor-in-Chief

New Directions for Methodology of Social and Behavioral Science
Donald W. Fiske, Editor-in-Chief

New Directions for Program Evaluation
Scarvia B. Anderson, Editor-in-Chief

New Directions for Student Services
Ursula Delworth and Gary R. Hanson, Editors-in-Chief

New Directions for Teaching and Learning
Kenneth E. Eble and John F. Noonan, Editors-in-Chief

New Directions for Testing and Measurement
William B. Schrader, Editor-in-Chief